THE BEARDED BRIDE

A CRITICAL EDITION OF

ÞRYMLUR

EDITED AND TRANSLATED BY
LEE COLWILL AND HAUKUR ÞORGEIRSSON

VIKING SOCIETY FOR NORTHERN RESEARCH
UNIVERSITY COLLEGE LONDON
2020

VIKING SOCIETY TEXTS

General Editors
Alison Finlay
Carl Phelpstead

© Viking Society for Northern Research 2020
Printed by Short Run Press Limited, Exeter

ISBN: 978-0-903521-98-7

Cover image: 'Ah, what a lovely maid it is!' by Elmer Boyd Smith. From Abbie Farwell Brown, 1902. *In the Days of Giants: A Book of Norse Tales* (Boston and New York: Houghton, Mifflin & Co), 122.

CONTENTS

INTRODUCTION
- 1. The rímur genre v
- 2. The manuscript and the scribe viii
- 3. Oral preservation viii
- 4. Dating and authorship ix
- 5. Poetic language xi
- 6. Metre xii
- 7. Parallels xvii
- 8. Previous editions xl
- 9. About this edition xl

ÞRYMLUR TEXT AND TRANSLATION 1

GLOSSARY 33

LIST OF NAMES 52

LIST OF MANUSCRIPTS 55

BIBLIOGRAPHY 55

INTRODUCTION

This book is a new critical edition of the Icelandic *rímur* cycle *Þrymlur*, which is preserved in a sixteenth-century manuscript but was probably composed around the year 1400. The poem tells the story of the theft of Þórr's hammer by the giant Þrymr and how Þórr must dress as a bride to reclaim it. This story is also found in two other sources: the Eddic poem *Þrymskviða* and a ballad known in different versions from Denmark, Norway, Sweden and the Faroe Islands.

Þrymlur constitutes the longest version of this story and includes a number of details not found elsewhere. To mention a few, Þórr is described as 'eight ells and twelve from head to toe' while Loki is referred to as Óðinn's 'servant' and 'slave'. When the gods travel to the land of the giants they are followed by an assortment of natural and supernatural creatures including 'very many goats and calves'. Þórr's hammer cannot be moved by a hundred men but an old giantess can carry it on her own. Finally, the coarseness of the wedding party is emphasised and lingered over, as is the violent dénouement.

This edition closely reflects the poem's only extant manuscript, while also adding an extensive commentary on the text, as well as an introduction placing *Þrymlur* in a wider context of poetic compositions about the theft of Þórr's hammer and stories which make use of the same folktale motifs.

The edition includes a translation into English, the first translation of *Þrymlur* into another language, with the aim of making this interesting example of Norse mythology in the late medieval period accessible to a wider range of readers.

1. The *rímur* genre

The *rímur* genre seems to have developed in Iceland around the beginning of the fourteenth century. The earliest extant example is *Óláfs ríma Haraldssonar*, found in Flateyjarbók and attributed there to the lawman Einarr Gilsson. Flateyjarbók itself dates to *c*.1387–94, but Einarr is known to have been the lawman in Northern Iceland for the year 1367–68, making it probable that the *ríma* predates the manuscript by some years (Stefán Karlsson 1970, 298–99). Moreover, the rubric in Flateyjarbók refers to this text as a *ríma* in the apparent certainty that its audience would recognise the term, suggesting that the genre was already well-established prior to the manuscript's creation. *Óláfs ríma* is unusually short by the standards of medieval *rímur*, consisting of only a single *ríma* ('canto' or 'fit') of sixty-five stanzas. More commonly medieval *rímur* consist of multiple fits (an average of eight or so), with the stanzas per fit numbering anywhere from in the twenties to over one hundred (Jorgensen 1993, 536). The corpus of medieval *rímur* is small when compared to the large number composed after the Reformation—it is difficult to give a precise number, partly because of the disagreement over what constitutes 'medieval' in an Icelandic context, and partly because many *rímur* are preserved in manuscripts younger than their apparent date of composition, but Finnur Sigmundsson's *Rímnatal* lists seventy-eight pre-1600 *rímur*, compared to almost twice that from the seventeenth century, and almost twice that again from the eighteenth.

Rímur are distinguished from earlier forms of Icelandic poetry primarily by their use of end-rhyme as an integral part of their metre. Whilst many *rímur* are anonymous, enough are attributed to named poets to make it probable that there were not the same expectations of anonymity, of speaking with the voice of common wisdom, that are seen in Eddic poetry. *Rímur* are equally unlike skaldic poetry; though they inherit its complicated poetic language and formal virtuosity, *rímur* are essentially narrative. *Rímur* associated with named patrons are a rarity, unlike skaldic poems, although some are known. For example, Jón lærði Guðmundsson's *Grænlandsannáll* (1623) claims that Einarr fóstri composed *Skíða ríma* for his patron Björn Jórsalafari as part of a contract to entertain him on particular days. It is more common to find *rímur* dedicated to women as part of their *mansöngvar*. These are stanzas found at the head of each individual *ríma* in which the poet addresses the woman or women they hope to impress by composing the *rímur*. It is not always clear to what extent these should be read as reflecting real relationships, as opposed to merely fulfilling a poetic convention. It is worth noting that the very earliest *ríma*, *Óláfs ríma*, does not contain *mansöngvar*, nor are they apparent in *Þrymlur*, although something may have been lost along with the start of the poem; here the poet's final stanza covers some of the same ground in its request that the audience respect poetry and not cast it aside. For an overview of the development of *mansöngvar* in the *rímur* tradition, see Hans Kuhn's 1990–93 article, 'The *rímur*-poet and his audience'.

Before the Reformation, *rímur* tended not to be attributed to named poets. There are a handful of exceptions, most notably Einarr Gilsson's *Óláfs ríma*, and poetry collectors of the seventeenth century onwards were inclined to credit known *rímur* poets with a variety of works, not always accurately (Ármann Jakobsson 2014). The named pre-Reformation *rímur* poets are all men; although the poet of *Landrés rímur* was female, her name is unknown (Louis-Jensen 1992). From the latter half of the sixteenth century, the number of extant *rímur* increases sharply, and it becomes far more common for poets to identify themselves in their poetry, though often in deliberately cryptic form. The vast majority of known poets are still men, but several female poets are known from the seventeenth and eighteenth centuries (Finnur Sigmundsson 1966, II 189–98).

That the development of *rímur* was influenced by foreign poetic traditions is undeniable, although opinion differs as to the precise source and nature of this influence. Björn K. Þórólfsson argues that the four-line stanza characteristic of most *rímur* metres is the product of influence from the traditional ballads of the British Isles and Scandinavia (Björn K. Þórólfsson 1934, 53). Vésteinn Ólason, however, maintains that the *rímur* genre was established in Iceland before ballads reached its shores, and that the main influence on the genre was instead that of Continental, especially Middle English, narrative poetry. He also notes the similarity of subject matter between the *rímur*, whose earliest incarnations frequently rework the chivalric sagas, and the French *chansons de geste* (Vésteinn Ólason 1982, 64–77). Recent scholarship (e.g. Hughes 2005, 206) has tended to concur with Vésteinn's position.

Though the *rímur* show distinct signs of foreign influence, they are also to some extent the natural descendants of earlier forms of Icelandic poetry. The vast majority of *rímur* make use of the kennings and *heiti* common in skaldic verse, and as the tradition develops, the kennings used grow more and more elaborate. Vésteinn Ólason has argued that as *rímur* poets tended not to strive for originality in their subject matter, this use of ornate periphrasis was the main means by which *rímur* poets could distinguish themselves from the competition (Vésteinn Ólason 1982, 53). Björn K. Þórólfsson has also argued for a strong continuity of form between the *dróttkvætt* metres of skaldic verse and the newer *ferskeytt* metre that was most popular in early *rímur* (Björn K. Þórólfsson 1950).

Their choice of subject matter, too, places the *rímur* squarely in a continuous tradition of Icelandic literature. It is extremely rare for *rímur* poets to create a new story for their poetry—of the pre-1600 *rímur*, only *Skíða ríma* and *Fjósa ríma* seem not to be based on any antecedent (Jorgensen 1993, 536)—although in some cases the source-texts no longer survive. The most popular sources of inspiration for the *rímur* seem to have been *fornaldarsögur* and *riddarasögur*. This is a pattern that is established in the late-medieval *rímur* and persists through to the nineteenth century. *Þrymlur* is highly unusual in apparently being based on another poetic work, *Þrymskviða*. It is far more common for *rímur* poets to refashion a prose tale as poetry.

2. The manuscript and the scribe

Þrymlur is a *rímur* cycle now preserved only in one mid-sixteenth-century Icelandic manuscript, Staðarhólsbók (AM 604 4to), a large collection of medieval *rímur* (Rósa Þorsteinsdóttir 2013). Another fragmentary manuscript was in Árni Magnússon's possession, but was lost at some point after 1730 without any surviving copies (Jón Helgason 1975, 241–42). Originally Staðarhólsbók was one unusually thick book of approximately 280 leaves containing thirty-three *rímur* cycles, but at some point after 1728 the book was divided into eight booklets of modest size containing a total of 248 leaves. Thirty or so leaves are lost. The booklet containing Þrymlur has the shelfmark AM 604 g 4to; Þrymlur is found on ff. 14r–15v.

The book is written by the same scribe throughout, Tómas Arason, son of Ari Jónsson who was a priest from Súgandafjörður in the Westfjords. Ari and his sons were productive scribes who wrote in a consistent, neat, traditional style (Karl Óskar Ólafsson 2006). Tómas has left a substantial amount of marginalia consisting of proverbs, quatrains, appeals to saints, complaints about eye pain, notes on the quality of the ink and (unfounded) remarks on the poor quality of his own writing (Schott 2010, 64–101).

The sources of Staðarhólsbók are unknown but it seems likely that it is a compilation based on multiple source manuscripts containing smaller *rímur* collections or individual *rímur* cycles. The two cycles following Þrymlur in the manuscript are *Lokrur* and *Völsungs rímur*, both also containing mythological material. It is possible that all three came from the same source, but also conceivable that Tómas arranged them together in his collection because of their related subject material.

In its preserved form, Þrymlur consists of seventy-nine stanzas, divided into three fits. The first fit is defective at the beginning since a page has been lost from the manuscript. The text is otherwise intact and legible.

3. Oral preservation

The preserved text of Þrymlur has characteristics which are indicative of oral transmission, as previously argued by Jón Helgason (1975). In particular, there are multiple occasions where the order of the stanzas seems to have become jumbled: most obviously, stanza I.5 is out of place, and stanzas II.9–13 would benefit from rearrangement. There are also cases where individual stanzas would become more lucid if lines 3–4 were placed before lines 1–2 (e.g. I.3, III.9). As Jón Helgason notes, fluidity in the order of material is typical of oral tradition. It is also likely that some stanzas were forgotten in the oral stage, which might explain some of the overly terse parts of the narrative.

We do not think it likely that Tómas wrote down *Þrymlur* directly from oral recitation or his own memory, since the text has many errors which seem characteristic of scribal transmission—for example III.11.3 <grett>, which fails to rhyme with <huertt> in the following line, or II.19.2 <grimmre>, which is too meaningless to thrive in oral preservation but an easy mistake to make when copying.

4. Dating and authorship

Being preserved in Staðarhólsbók, *Þrymlur* can clearly be no younger than the mid-sixteenth century. Apart from this, the text can be dated only by internal arguments based on language and style. In previous studies of medieval *rímur*, the cycle has been placed among the oldest preserved texts. In Björn Karel Þórólfsson's study, the work is placed in the category 'oldest *rímur*' as the eighth oldest cycle (Björn K. Þórólfsson 1934, 294–390; 312–14). In a study by Haukur Þorgeirsson, *Þrymlur* is also placed in the oldest group, here dated to the period 1350–1400, as the sixth oldest cycle (Haukur Þorgeirsson 2013, 249). Neither study, however, explicitly presents arguments for the dating of individual cycles.

The main linguistic argument for giving *Þrymlur* an early date is the absence of clearly young rhymes. Many *rímur* cycles in Staðarhólsbók have occurrences of rhyme between the originally rounded vowels *y/ý/ey* and their unrounded counterparts *i/í/ei*. This can be taken as an indicator of relatively young age—from the second half of the fifteenth century and later. There are, however, no rhymes of this type in *Þrymlur*, in which the rounded and unrounded vowels are consistently kept apart (e.g. I.9 *fleiri-meiri*; II.4 *geima-heima-þeima*; III.23 *brýtr-hrýtr*). An even more archaic feature is that there are no rhymes between *e* and *é*, something which becomes common even before the unrounding of *y/ý/ey*. In *Þrymlur*, *e* and *é* are consistently kept apart in rhyme (e.g. I.3 *vel-hel*, *pretta-þetta*; I.6 *lét-hét*; I.22 *sléttum-fréttum*).

The poet twice rhymes old *vá* with *á* (I.9 *svá-þá* and III.18 *vár-tár*), a relatively archaic trait which becomes much less common *c*.1500. The rhyme *vóru-fóru* (I.14) does not disrupt this pattern since the form *vóru* is an old one. Words with epenthetic *r* are never employed in disyllabic position at the end of a line, a further trait consistent with composition before the sixteenth century.

The vocabulary of the cycle is consistent with an early dating. Loanwords characteristic of the sixteenth century, such as *strax* and *soddan*, are not found. Nor are there examples of words like *par*, *art*, *þenkja*, *lukka*, *finn* and *kvintr* which had already become common in the fifteenth century.

There are, however, three rhyme pairs which might be taken to indicate that the cycle is not among the very oldest. The simplification of certain double final consonants is a development which began in the fourteenth century and continued in the fifteenth. This trait might be present in stanza I.4 which rhymes (in normalised spelling) *mjór* with *Þórr*, possibly indicating that the nominative *Þórr* has been simplified to *Þór*. But there is another possible explanation: the poet could have used analogical nominative forms like *mjórr* with a double consonant. This is the norm in the mid-fourteenth-century Möðruvallabók (de Leeuw van Weenen 2000, 143), so would not be a young trait in the *rímur* context. Another possible case is stanza I.12 where *stórr* seems to rhyme with *fór*, with *stórr* agreeing with *halrinn*. However, the adjective could also be taken to agree with *heimboð*, in which case the rhyme is *stór-fór*. In other cases the poet does not conflate final *rr* with *r*, rhyming on one hand I.13 *stór-Þór*, I.23 *fór-Þór*, III.1 *svör-för*, III.8 *stór-Þór*, III.18 *vár-tár* and on the other hand III.12 *kurr-burr*, III.22 *stórr-Þórr* and III.25 *Þórr-stórr*.

A third possible case of simplification of final consonants is in stanza I.21 where nominative *dæll* seems to rhyme with dative *þræl*—though both words are written with double *l* in the manuscript. The simplification of final *ll* was never carried out consistently, and may have been a dialectal feature, making it more difficult to evaluate as chronological evidence. Nevertheless, this is a possible case of a young feature, perhaps suggesting an origin in the fifteenth rather than the fourteenth century.

The short length of *Þrymlur* makes dating the cycle more uncertain. Based on the linguistic data, we offer the period 1350–1450 as the most likely time of composition.

Nothing is known about the author of *Þrymlur*. Many *rímur* cycles have introductory stanzas (*mansöngr*) where the poet gives some personal information, but if *Þrymlur* ever had such stanzas they are lost with the beginning of the first *ríma*. Thus, even the gender of the poet is unknown. Most *rímur* cycles appear to have been composed by men but there is one case of known female authorship for a medieval cycle (*Landrés rímur*, see Louis-Jensen 1992) and nothing in particular rules this out for *Þrymlur*.

It is possible that future stylometric research could build a case that the anonymous author of *Þrymlur* also composed some other preserved *rímur* cycle. The most promising cycle for comparison may be *Lokrur*, which shares some of the same vocabulary. The similarities might, however, be due to a shared interest in mythology rather than common authorship.

5. Poetic language

The poetic language of *Þrymlur* is relatively straightforward and typical of early *rímur*. Kennings are used sparingly. The following examples are traditional and unproblematic:

woman: *þella veiga* (II.2.1), *gullhlaðs skorða* (II.3.1), *þorna Gefn* (II.5.1), *hringa Fríðr* (II.12.3), *lauka rein* (III.4.1), *menja Bil* (III.17.2)

gold: *Ofnis skíði* (II.12.1), *Gefnar tár* (III.18.4)

Þórr: *Herjans burr* (I.5.2, I.7.2), *Rögnis kundr* (I.29.1), *Fjölnis burr* (II.1.3)

man: *örva Þundr* (I.10.1)

poetry: *Herjans snekkja* (II.1.1)

sword: *hjalta kólfr* (I.5.1)

hands: *hauka fold* (I.11.2)

Loki is referred to as *Fjölnis þjón* (I.21.1), *Óðins þræl* (I.21.3) and *nála burr* (III.12). The first two constructions are paralleled in *Lokrur*.

More challenging are **Grímnis kundr* (= Þórr, I.10.3) and *bauga *eyja* (= woman, II.22.1) where we have resorted to emendation to obtain normal kennings. Further difficult constructions include *beiti sára* (II.13.1), *fleina rógum* (II.15.1) and **landa baugr* (I.21.2). Inaccurate transmission is probably to blame for some or all of these difficulties. Each kenning is discussed further in the notes to individual stanzas.

A number of *heiti* (conventional poetic words) are used, particularly for men (*halr, seggr, ýtar, beimar, höldar, bragnar, rekkar*) or people (*dróttir*) and women (*víf, sprund, fljóð, drós*). The gods are referred to by multiple traditional names:

Óðinn: *Rögnir* (I.26.2, I.29.1, II.7.2), *Herjann* (I.5.2, I.7.2, II.1.1), *Fjölnir* (I.21.1, II.1.3), *Grímnir* (by emendation, I.10.3)

Loki: *Loftr* (I.1.4, I.19.3, III.1.3, III.4.1, III.12.1), *Lóður* (I.22.3)

Þórr: *Atli* (I.6.1, II.5.2), *Rymr* (II.6.3, III.26.1)

A potential source of confusion is the poet's practice of referring to Þrymr by generic giant names and then using the same giant names for apparently separate characters. Thus, *Dofri* (I.24.2) and *Brúsi* (II.22.1) refer to Þrymr but also seem to be the names of wedding guests in stanza III.6.4. Even worse, *Grímnir* seems to refer once to Óðinn (I.10.3), once to Þrymr (II.19.2) and once to a separate giant (III.6.4). To be sure, two of these cases rely on emendation.

6. Metre

(i) *The three metres*

It is normal in *rímur* for the poet to change metres with every fit, and this is the case in *Þrymlur*. The first fit is composed in *ferskeytt*, the most common *rímur* metre and the one almost universally used for the first fit of a cycle. Each stanza consists of four lines. Lines 1 and 3 have seven metrical positions, terminating in monosyllabic rhyme. Lines 2 and 4 have six metrical positions, terminating in disyllabic rhyme. Additionally, the even lines may optionally begin with anacrusis (an extrametrical unstressed position). Anacrusis in the odd lines is rare in *ferskeytt* and there are no instances of it in *Þrymlur*. Schematically, a *ferskeytt* stanza can be represented as follows, where S represents a strong metrical position and W a weak one:

(W) S W S W S W S
(W) S W S W S W
(W) S W S W S W S
(W) S W S W S W

The second fit is composed in *braghent*, where the first line has twelve metrical positions and lines 2–3 have eight. Anacrusis is possible in each line but there are only two instances in *Þrymlur* (II.3.1, II.11.3). The first line sometimes has a caesura after the fourth strong position. This is obvious in stanzas II.19 and II.20 where it is indicated in the manuscript. It is also clear in stanzas II.10 and II.11, which would otherwise be unmetrical. We can represent the metre as follows:

(W) S W S W S W S (W) S W S W
(W) S W S W S W S W
(W) S W S W S W S W

The third metre is *stafhent*. Each line has seven metrical positions, terminating in monosyllabic rhyme. Anacrusis is allowed but uncommon in *Þrymlur*. The scheme is as follows:

(W) S W S W S W S
(W) S W S W S W S
(W) S W S W S W S
(W) S W S W S W S

(ii) *Placement of alliteration*

All *rímur* metres have structural alliteration which is manifested in similar ways in the different metres. In *ferskeytt*, each half-stanza must have three alliterating strong positions. One must be the third strong position in the odd line and one must be the first strong position in the even line. The remaining alliterator can be freely placed in the first, second or fourth strong position in the odd line. The first position is the most popular choice. This can be represented as follows:

Ferskeytt:

(W) **S** W S W <u>S</u> W **S**
(W) <u>S</u> W S W S W

Stafhent:

(W) **S** W S W <u>S</u> W **S**
(W) <u>S</u> W S W S W S

The underlined positions must carry alliteration and at least one of the positions in bold must as well. Alliteration in *braghent* can be represented as follows:

(W) **S** W S W <u>S</u> W **S** (W) <u>S</u> W S W
(W) **S** W S W <u>S</u> W S W
(W) **S** W S W S W S W

At first glance the initial line may appear anomalous, but if the optional caesura after the third strong position is kept in mind it is easier to reconcile it with the general pattern. Note line II.19.1 where the caesura is represented with a dot in the manuscript:

Þegnum heilsar þussa gramur. þrymur j kife.

We could represent this as two lines:

Þegnum heilsar þussa gramur.
þrymur j kife.

In this representation, the alliterators fall on the first and third strong positions in the odd line and the first strong position of the even line, exactly the same pattern as elsewhere.

(iii) *Hyperalliteration and additional alliteration*

Up to around 1300, Icelandic poetry rigidly observed a stricture against hyperalliteration (the occurrence of more than three alliterative words in a set). It also scrupulously avoided additional alliteration (the presence of alliterating word pairs outside the mandatory structural alliteration). These strictures were weakened in the fourteenth century (Ragnar Ingi Aðalsteinsson 2014), and by the time of the *rímur*, the poets no longer seem to make an effort to avoid this—and this is true of *Þrymlur*.

Two examples of hyperalliteration:

> Loki var **k**læddur **k**vinnu **k**læðum.
> **K**lókur þótti hann næsta í ræðum. (II.10)
>
> **S**eggir tóku að **s**egja í **s**enn:
> '**S**áld af mjöðinum drakk hon enn!' (III.17)

There are two additional instances in stanzas II.23 and III.26.

Four examples of additional alliteration:

> **H**eimboð veitti **h**alrinn stórr
> **h**ölda **s**veit með **s**igri. (I.12)
>
> Óðinn átti **f**rábært **f**ar er **f**lutti beima. (II.11)
>
> **S**íðan **s**ettist **b**rúðr á **b**ekk.
> **B**augi allt til **v**eizlu fekk. (III.3)
>
> **S**íðan **l**emr hann **t**röllin **t**ólf.
> **T**ennur **h**rjóta um **h**allar **g**ólf. (III.24)

There are additional instances in stanzas I.9, I.17, III.4, III.8 and III.13.

(iv) *Equivalence classes in alliteration*

For the most part, each initial consonant forms its own equivalence class, regardless of the following phonemes. For example *glófar*, *görpum* and *greyptir* alliterate together in stanza I.11. However, /s/ behaves exceptionally in that /st/, /sk/ and /sp/ each form a class of their own, separate from the main /s/ class. For some medieval *rímur* the same is true for /sl/ and /sn/. *Þrymlur*, as it happens, has no examples bearing on this.

All vowel-initial words belong to the same equivalence class. For example, *æðir*, *illsku* and *allur* alliterate together in stanza I.27. The old tradition of /j/-initial words alliterating with vowels is still upheld in many medieval *rímur*, including *Þrymlur*.

(v) *Rhyme*

Each *ferskeytt* stanza contains two monosyllabic words rhyming together and two disyllabic words rhyming together. Each *braghent* stanza has three disyllabic words rhyming. Each *stafhent* stanza has two pairs of monosyllabic rhyme.

The rhyme in *rímur* is normally exact and identical rhyme is avoided. In three cases (I.6, I.16, III.1), the manuscript text has defective rhyme and we have emended it to perfect rhyme. In two cases (II.10, II.15) we have not emended the text despite imperfect rhyme, since no clear solution presents itself. In two cases (III.9, III.18), original /vá/ rhymes with /á/

despite phonological changes which have caused the vowel to be written as <o> (see further Hreinn Benediktsson 2002).

In keeping with restrictions observed in all medieval *rímur*, disyllabic words at the end of a line never include the definite article or epenthetic /u/ (Haukur Þorgeirsson 2013).

(vi) *Stress and syllable quantity*

It is convenient to think of the trochee, a strong metrical position followed by a weak one, as the basic building block of the *rímur* metres. Each line of a *ferskeytt* stanza contains three trochees and the odd lines contain an additional stressed final syllable. A trochee is most simply formed as a disyllabic word with a heavy first syllable, as in this example:

> Glófar vinna görpum mein
> greyptir hauka foldu

The first syllables have a long vowel followed by one or more consonants (*glófar*, *greyptir*, *hauka*), or a short vowel followed by a long consonant (*vinna*) or a consonant cluster (*görpum*, *foldu*).

When the initial syllable of a disyllabic word is short it cannot form a metrical trochee on its own, but along with the next syllable it can form a strong metrical position in a process known as resolution. For example *borið hann* (III.21.4), *þegar að* (III.17) and *fáumst vér* (III.14) form trochees: the strong position is occupied by *borið*, *þegar* and *fáumst* while the weak position is occupied by the subsequent word. By the same process, words like *hamarinn* (III.21.1), *gripirnir* (I.9.2) and *höfuðið* (III.26.4) form acceptable trochees on their own.

A weak metrical position can also be occupied by two syllables if the first syllable is light. This is known as neutralisation. In III.20.2 we have *hamar fyrir* as a trochee. The strong position is occupied by two syllables through resolution while the weak position is occupied by two syllables through neutralisation. By the same token, words like *höllina* (III.22.1) and *byrlara* (III.16.3) form acceptable trochees.

Trisyllabic words which have a heavy first and second syllable, like *höfðinginn* (III.6.2) cannot form a trochee and must instead occupy three metrical positions.

For a monosyllabic word followed by an unstressed word, the weight of the initial syllable can depend on whether the following word begins with a vowel or a consonant. For example, *þá mun* (I.25.3) forms an acceptable trochee since the initial *m* of *mun* helps lend weight to the initial syllable. The same is true for *hvar sem* (I.14.2). Combinations like *þá er* or *hvar er* would not form full trochees but can form one stressed position by resolution, as in this line:

Hvar er hann Mjöllnir fólginn? (I.27.4)

Here, *hvar er* occupies a strong position and *hann* occupies a weak position. Dropping *hann* would be semantically acceptable but leave the line unmetrical.

Elision is to be assumed in cases like *færi eg* (I.28.1) and *þóttu úr* (II.6.2) where the first syllable is heavy, but it is presumably disallowed in cases like *fara í* (II.4.2) and *drifu úr* (II.7.2) where the first syllable is light.

Epenthetic *u* is normally present in the manuscript, but the metrics tell a more complicated story. Words which are disyllabic in Modern Icelandic and have epenthetic *u* are consistently used in monosyllabic rhyme in the medieval *rímur*. Examples from *Þrymlur*, in the spelling of the manuscript, include <ullur>–<fullur> (I.1) and <dægur>–<slægur> (III.2), which we have normalised as *ullr-fullr* and *dægr-slægr*. Within the line we have normalised the words as having epenthetic *u* unless followed by an unstressed vowel: hence <klokur> becomes *klókur* (II.10.3) and <rymur uid> becomes *Rymur við* but <brvdurenn> becomes *brúðrin* (III.4.4) and <nidur j> becomes *niðr í* (III.20.3).

By the mid-sixteenth century the distinction between light and heavy syllables was in the process of disappearing. As it happens, our scribe, Tómas Arason, has left us some stanzas of his own and from this we can evaluate his own position in this development. In the five stanzas added by him at the end of *Skáld-Helga rímur* there are five hypometric trochees: 1.1 *guð hann*, 2.1 *segið*, 2.4 *guð oss*, 4.2 *hefur*, 5.4 *þikir* (*Rs* I:162–63). This suggests that the quantity distinction was largely lost from his language (or at least from his poetic sensibilities). This in turn may have made him more prone to certain mistakes in copying, such as omitting words which were metrically but not semantically necessary.

We can verify this suspicion by a comparison with a *rímur* cycle which is preserved in more manuscripts. *Ormars rímur* is preserved in three old manuscripts, each independent of the others, and one of them is Staðarhólsbók. In this text there are at least five cases where Tómas has created a hypometric line by omitting a monosyllabic pronoun present in the other manuscripts (I.5.3, I.5.4, III.41.1, IV.4.3, IV.7.4; Haukur Þorgeirsson 2013, 279–318). Since *Ormars rímur* are a bit more than twice the length of *Þrymlur* we would expect two or so examples of this in the latter cycle. Metrical problems like the defective trochee *hvað að* in *Þrymlur* I.15.3 may be a result of similar omissions by our scribe.

7. Parallels

The story of the theft of the thunder-god's instrument of power (ATU 1148b in the Aarne-Thompson-Uther folktale motif-index) is found throughout the Circum-Baltic region, transcending linguistic and cultural barriers between Finno-Ugric and Indo-European groups (Frog 2011; Vijūnas 2019). The motif of the substituted bride (K1911 in the Thompson motif-index), meanwhile, is even more widespread, with a variant bearing striking similarities to the narrative of *Þrymlur* known from the Arabic world from perhaps as early as the fourteenth century (Paret 1930, 112–14; Singer 1932, 47–48). Within the Nordic cultural sphere, a narrative encompassing both these motifs appears in several distinct forms, the earliest attested and best known of which is the Eddic poem *Þrymskviða*. The narrative later appears in other poetic genres, namely the *rímur* which are the subject of the present work, and a number of ballads from continental Scandinavia, some of which were not committed to writing until the end of the nineteenth century (Bugge and Moe 1897). This section will give an overview of the main points of similarity and difference between these variants, with emphasis on the Scandinavian tradition.

(i) *Folktale motifs*

Tale-type ATU 1148b may be summarised as follows: While the thunder-god sleeps, his instruments of power are stolen by malevolent beings (variously devils or ogres). In the process of retrieving them, the god dons a humiliating disguise. In the non-Scandinavian Circum-Baltic traditions, he is usually disguised as a servant or other person of low rank. In the ballads and Icelandic poetry, he is disguised as a bride. The disguised god arrives at the location to which the instruments have been taken. There is frequently a scene in which the thief or his household is unable to use the instruments. The disguised god is then freely given the instrument, at which point he successfully uses it to drive away, injure or kill those who stole it (Frog 2011, 78). Outside Scandinavia, this tale is primarily preserved in prose oral accounts, most of which were not fixed in writing until the nineteenth or twentieth centuries. It is therefore extremely difficult to draw any definite conclusions about the extent to which the various tales interacted with and were influenced by one another.

Although the substitute-bride motif (ATU 403c) is widely attested, in its more usual form it is a malevolent entity that performs the deception, killing or banishing the rightful bride and deceiving an innocent husband (Uther 2004, 238). Nevertheless, Inger Margrethe Boberg identifies *Þrymskviða* as being a variant on this motif, and it therefore follows that

Þrymlur and the ballads, all of which ultimately descend from either *Þrymskviða* or its underlying narrative, should also be identified with it (Boberg 1966, 183).

In this more specific variant, the protagonist disguises himself as a bride in order to save a woman from marriage to a monster. This is the motif identified by Samuel Singer in an Arabic folktale, preserved in manuscripts from the eighteenth century, but potentially as old as the fourteenth century (Paret 1930, 112; Singer 1932, 47). In this tale Ali, the Prophet's son-in-law, disguises himself as a bride in order to deceive a giant who wishes to marry a merchant's daughter. Under the disguise, the bride's unusual strength and flashing eyes are commented on, in a way comparable to the comments on 'Freyja's' prodigious appetite and *ǫndótt* eyes in both *Þrymskviða* and *Þrymlur*. Ali's companions play a similar role to Loki in distracting their suspicious host with flattery. As in the Scandinavian tales, the narrative concludes with the disguised protagonist slaughtering the giant's household before making his escape (Singer 1932, 47–48).

An episode in the late-medieval romance *Samsons saga fagra* may also be identified with this motif, although here neither the groom nor the 'bride' may be said to have pure motives (Wilson, ed., 1953, 43–45).[1] Here, King Sigurðr desires to marry the young and beautiful Hrafnaborg, although people comment that his son is far more suitable for her in terms of age. Just before the wedding is due to take place, however, the bride-to-be encounters the thief Kvinntelinn while hunting in a nearby forest. She and her maid are put to sleep and Kvinntelinn dons her clothes and attends the wedding in her place. During the ceremony, Sigurðr arrays his bride in a magical cloak that can detect an unfaithful wife (cf. *Mǫttuls saga*) and gives her a sceptre. Kvinntelinn uses the sceptre to knock the king down and makes his escape with both sceptre and cloak. The parallels between this and the *Þrymskviða* narrative are readily apparent. The earliest manuscript containing *Samsons saga*, AM 343 a 4to, dates from c.1450–75 (Sanders 2000, 42–43), and it seems likely that its author was influenced by the story of Þórr and his hammer, whether that influence came by way of *Þrymskviða* itself or *Þrymlur*, or in the more nebulous form of oral tradition.

Elements of the *Þrymskviða* material also resurface in an etiological folktale concerning the farm at Urebø, in Norway (*DgF*, IV 582–83). This tale is first attested in a manuscript from 1777 (NKS 1568 4to), and features a *bjærgtrold* 'mountain-giant' by the name of 'Tor Troll-bane'.

---

[1] We are grateful to Jonathan Hui for drawing our attention to this parallel.

This Tor attends a wedding feast, but the wedding guests, wishing to save some of the feast for themselves, refuse to satisfy his enormous appetite and Tor becomes angry. One good-hearted man brings Tor home with him and gives him plenty of ale. This is not enough to appease Tor, and he uses his hammer to crush the nearby mountain, sparing only the generous man. This deed proves too much for the hammer, however, which flies off its shaft and is lost. The good man makes Tor promise that if he finds it again, he will make a path for the local people to use. The hammer is recovered and Tor keeps his promise. Given the appearance of a Þórr figure who overeats at a wedding feast, in addition to the loss of (a part of) his hammer, this tale almost certainly bears some relation to the *Þrymskviða* material.

This goes some way to demonstrating the widespread popularity of many of the motifs that make up the story told in *Þrymskviða*. It is therefore hardly surprising that, when brought together in a single text, the tale should have been subject to numerous retellings.

(ii) *Þrymlur* and *Þrymskviða*

Both of the above tale types are evident in *Þrymlur*, which follows the basic narrative of *Þrymskviða* almost exactly. Following a feast at Þórr's hall, the hammer 'disappears' through trickery. Upon enquiry, Loki learns that the giant Þrymr has concealed it underground and will only return it in exchange for Freyja as a bride. Freyja, unsurprisingly, refuses this deal and Heimdæll (as he is called here) proposes that Þórr take her place. Though the false bride's appetite awakens the giants' suspicions, the hammer is nonetheless brought in, whereupon the 'maiden' seizes it and deals violently with the thieves.

Even from this brief summary, however, some degree of variation is apparent. *Þrymskviða* famously starts *in medias res*, with no explanation of who Þórr is or why the audience should be concerned that his hammer has disappeared. The implicit assumption is that the audience is at least somewhat familiar with the story, and certainly with its central characters. As Margaret Clunies Ross (2002, 181) points out, much of the poem's comedic incongruity is lost if the audience is not already aware of Þórr's reputation as the big, bearded bouncer of Ásgarðr. Likewise, Freyja's protest that she will be called *vergjǫrnust* 'most man-eager' if she marries Þrymr can only be read ironically if the audience is familiar with other stories, such as those in *Lokasenna* and *Sǫrla þáttr*, in which she is said to have slept with almost every humanoid male in the mythological world (*Flateyjarbók* 1944, I 304; *Eddukvæði*, I 414).

In contrast to *Þrymskviða*'s dramatic opening, *Þrymlur* begins more sedately, with a brief overview of those gods who will figure prominently in the rest of the *rímur*. Owing to the lacuna in the manuscript, the extant poem opens partway through a stanza on the 'famous' Ullr, but judging by the lengths of the three *rímur* (29, 23 and 27 stanzas respectively, in their extant forms), it seems unlikely that a great deal of material has been lost. The surviving introduction seems designed to give an audience who, at least four centuries after the Conversion, might have had only a passing familiarity with the characters, a reminder of the major players' key characteristics. The material which the *rímur* poet chooses to include in this section all contributes to the audience's deeper appreciation of the story. For example, Loki's introduction emphasises his highly ambivalent nature. His monstrous offspring are enumerated and their antipathy to the Æsir established. He is also described as *lymskufullr* 'full of cunning' (st.I.1) and capable of deceiving many *með slægðum* 'with slyness' (st.I.4), traits that will become important later when his quick thinking is needed to allay the giants' suspicions about Þórr's appetite.[2] Already, a certain fluidity in his approach to gender is apparent: the poet takes care to mention that *móðir sé hann að Sleipni* 'he is mother to Sleipnir' (st.I.2), and his physical appearance is described as *langr og mjór* 'long and thin' (st.I.4) in contrast to *undra digr* 'marvellously stout' (st.I.10) Þórr, perhaps to explain the ease with which he dons a female disguise later in the poem.

Meanwhile, Þórr's introductory stanzas emphasise both his impressive size (as previously mentioned, he is *undra digr*, but also *átta álna og tólf upp á höfuð af ristum* 'eight ells and twelve up to his head from his insteps' (st.I.6)), and his physical strength. Significantly, this strength is associated with physical objects: the hammer Mjöllnir, with which he fights giants, the girdles of strength, which make him stronger than trolls, and the gloves of steel that allow him to grip a stone as easily as if it were dirt. By externalising Þórr's strength in this way, the poet highlights its fragility as well as hammering home the centrality of Mjöllnir to Þórr's role as defender of the gods, in order that the audience be fully able to appreciate the significance of its disappearance when the time comes.

Although as a general rule the poet of *Þrymlur* tends to add detail to the account in *Þrymskviða*, there are also elements to which less attention

---

[2] All quotations from and references to *Þrymlur* are based on the text of this edition, with quotations given in normalised orthography. We have chosen to keep the stanza order seen in the manuscript and our stanza numbers therefore differ from those found in Finnur Jónsson's editions.

is paid. The cross-dressing episode is a notable example of this. Many scholars have commented on *Þrymskviða*'s anxieties surrounding the correct performance of gender (e.g. Clunies Ross 2002, 181–89; McKinnell 2014, 203), with the hammer Mjǫllnir often read as a phallic symbol whose disappearance represents a threat to Þórr's masculinity (Clunies Ross 2002, 181). It is therefore interesting to compare *Þrymskviða*'s treatment of Þórr's transformation with the same scene in *Þrymlur*.

Þrymskviða lingers over this episode. First, Heimdallr proposes the scheme, listing in detail the precise feminine accoutrements in which Þórr should be arrayed:

> 15. Þá kvað Heimdallr,
> hvítastr *ása,*
> vissi hann vel fram
> sem vanir aðrir:
> 'Bindu vér Þór þá
> brúðar líni,
> hafi hann it mikla
> men Brísinga.
>
> 16. Látum und honum
> hrynja lukla
> ok kvenváðir
> um kné falla,
> en *á brjósti*
> breiða steina,
> ok hagliga
> um hǫfuð typpum.'   (*Eddukvæði* I, 424)

> Then Heimdallr spoke,
> the whitest of the Æsir,
> he knew what lay ahead as well
> as the other Vanir do:
> 'Then we will bind Þórr
> with a bride's headdress,
> let him wear the great
> necklace of the Brísingar.
>
> Let us cause keys to rattle
> down from him
> and women's clothing
> to fall to his knees,
> and on his breast
> place broad stones,
> and neatly cover
> his head with a hood.'

After a brief interlude in which Þórr voices his objections to this plan, these stanzas are repeated almost word-for-word:

> 19. Bundu þeir Þór þá
> brúðar líni
> ok inu mikla
> meni Brísinga,
> létu und honum
> hrynja lukla
> ok kvenváðir
> um kné falla,
> en á brjósti
> breiða steina,
> ok hagliga
> um hǫfuð typpum.   (*Eddukvæði* I, 425)

> Then they bound Þórr
> with a bride's headdress
> and the great
> necklace of the Brísingar,
> they caused keys to rattle
> down from him
> and women's clothing
> to fall to his knees,
> and on his breast
> placed broad stones,
> and neatly covered
> his head with a hood.

This methodical repetition slows down the narrative, forcing the audience to confront and dwell on the ways in which gender can be externally imposed. The scene in *Þrymlur* is very different. Although it is not much shorter, there is none of the same attention to detail: the only specifics we are given regarding the transformation are that the Æsir *settu á bringu breiða steina, / blóðrautt gull og pellið hreina* 'set on his chest broad stones, blood-red gold and pure silk' (st.II.9). The repetition is entirely absent, save for the phrase *Ýtar bjuggu Ása-Þór* 'Men prepared Ása-Þórr' (st.II.9, II.12), which appears at the start of two stanzas. The verbal echo of *breiða steina* suggests that the poet of *Þrymlur* was familiar with the account given in *Þrymskviða*, but deliberately chose to take a different approach to the material.

Anxieties surrounding gender are in no way so apparent in *Þrymlur* as they are in *Þrymskviða*, in which Þórr explicitly voices his concerns, saying:

17. 'Mik munu Æsir
    argan kalla,
    ef ek bindask læt
    brúðar líni.' (*Eddukvæði* I, 425)
    'The Æsir will
    call me *argr*,[3]
    if I allow myself to be bound
    in a bride's headdress.'

This protest is nowhere to be found in *Þrymlur*, and indeed there is no suggestion that Þórr dressing as a woman will be harmful to anyone except the giants he deceives. Arguably, the poet pre-empts the audience's concerns about this scene with frequent reminders of how unlikely a bride Þórr is, with the incongruity of the disguise being returned to repeatedly over this section; for example, in II.12 we are told that *þessi karlinn kampa-síði / kemr í stað fyrir hringa Fríði* 'this long-whiskered man comes in place of the Fríðr of rings [= woman]', and in II.13, *Þórr er líki kvenna fára* 'Þórr is like few women'. These statements should also be read in light of Þórr's initial description as twenty ells high and 'marvellously stout'.

Whilst *Þrymlur* tones down concerns around gender, it plays up the violence and coarseness of the scenes in Jötunheimar. As the wedding feast gets under way, we are told that the giants leap up onto the benches (st.III.5), use their teeth instead of knives (st.III.8) and fight one another with such ferocity that *blóðið dreif um alla þá; / knútum var þar kastað oft. / Komu stundum hnefar á loft* 'the blood spattered all over them; knucklebones were often thrown there. Sometimes fists were raised' (st.III.9). 'Freyja's' appetite is also even more impressive here than in *Þrymskviða*, with eight salmon becoming twelve, on top of the usual oxen, mead and other delicacies (st.III.10). Finally, the violent dénouement, which in *Þrymskviða* is dispensed with in two stanzas, is lovingly lingered over here for four. Any detail lacking in the cross-dressing scene is made up for by the often gruesome emphasis on the precise nature of the giants' destruction:

    III.23 Sundur í miðju borðin brýtr;
        brauð og vín um gólfið hrýtr.

[3] Given the extensive debate over the precise translation of the word *argr*, it is left in the original here. The term connotes improper sexual behaviour and gender performance, which for men was often tantamount to a charge of being the receptive partner in penetrative sex. For an overview of the use of *argr* in Old Norse literature, see Meulengracht Sorensen 1983.

>   Jötnum versnar heldr í hug:
>   hjartað þeirra er komið á flug.
> III.24 Braut hann í sundr í Beslu hrygg.
>   Brúðrin fell þar eigi dygg.
>   Síðan lemr hann tröllin tólf.
>   Tennur hrjóta um hallar gólf.
> III.25 Æsiligur var Ása-Þórr.
>   Upp mun reiddur hamarinn stórr.
>   Setti hann niðr á Sauðungs kinn.
>   Sökk hann þegar í hausinn inn.
> III.26 Pústrað hefr hann pilta Rymr.
>   Prettum var leikinn skálkrinn Þrymr.
>   Hann fekk högg það hausinn tók.
>   Höfuðið fast með afli skók.
>
> He breaks the tables apart down the middle;
> bread and wine tumble to the floor.
> It gets rather worse for the giants in spirit:
> their hearts are ready to take flight.
>
> He broke apart Besla's spine.
> The unworthy woman fell there.
> Then he strikes twelve trolls.
> Teeth scattered across the hall floor.
>
> Ása-Þórr was violent.
> The huge hammer will be raised up.
> It came down on Sauðungur's cheek.
> It sank immediately into his skull.
>
> Rymr [=Þórr] has boxed boys' ears.
> The rogue Þrymr was deceived with tricks.
> He received a blow that took the skull.
> The head shook soundly with the force of the blow.

With the return of Mjöllnir, Þórr himself is returned to full power and this is something that the *rímur*-poet is keen to emphasise. Rather than the gender anxieties of *Þrymskviða*, *Þrymlur* concerns itself with the question of strength: who has it, how it can be taken, and, crucially, how it can be regained. The message is not, perhaps, delivered with a great deal of subtlety, but then arguably, neither is that of *Þrymskviða*.

The *rímur* genre, along with many of the other literary genres which flourished after the so-called Golden Age of Icelandic literature, has been rather marginalised for its perceived lack of subtlety, but when considering a text's approach to its source material, it is important to consider also the context in which such a text was received by its audience. Unfortunately, the performance contexts of both Eddic poetry and early *rímur* remain somewhat obscure. Terry Gunnell has suggested that dialogue-heavy poems such as *Þrymskviða* were suitable for performance by multiple actors in a form of early theatre; in this context, *Þrymskviða*'s focus on the external appearance of its characters may have aided its audience's identification of these characters with their respective actors (Gunnell 1995, 195). However, what little we know of the early performance of *rímur* suggests that this was not the case with later poetry. Unfortunately, our only detailed sources come from the sixteenth century or even later, but one of these, Oddur Einarsson's *Qualiscunque descriptio Islandiae* from the late sixteenth century, contains a fascinating description of what could conceivably be *rímur* performance at this time (Oddur Einarsson 1928, 66–67). In it Oddur describes the rhythmic chanting of poetry by a single speaker, to which the other inhabitants of the farm dance without singing. The idea of rhythmic chanting bears some similarity to the performance of *rímur* recorded by folklorists in the nineteenth and twentieth centuries.[4] Supporting the idea of *rímur* being performed at dances, Vésteinn Ólason points out that the poet of *Sörla rímur* specifically complains about people dancing too loudly to appreciate the artistry of the poetry (Vésteinn Ólason 1982, 40):

> Því má eg varla vísu slá
> veit eg það til sanns;
> þegar að rekkar rímu fá
> reyst er hún upp við dans.
>
> Gapa þeir upp og gumsa hart
> og geyma varla sín,
> höldar dansa hralla snart
> ef heyrist vísan mín.
>
> Thus I may scarcely strike up a verse,
> I know this for sure:
> as soon as the men get the rhyme
> it will be shouted out for a dance.
>
> They gape upwards and scoff hard
> and hardly control themselves,
> men dance hard and fast
> if my verse is heard.

Though it has been argued that most *rímur* are too long to dance to (Sverrir Tómasson 2012, 61), it is worth noting that the length of the fits in

---

[4] See ismus.is for examples.

Þrymlur are rather shorter than is usual; read aloud at a steady pace, the longest takes between three and four minutes, before concluding with a stanza or line which seems to signal a clear pause in the proceedings: *Falli þann veg ríma* 'May the *ríma* end in this way' (st.I.29) and *Þar mun bragrinn verða falla* 'There the poetry will have to cease' (st.II.23). In a performance context in which an audience was at least partly focused on dancing, it would be unsurprising if a poet dispensed with some subtleties. Such a performance context may also go some way to explaining *Þrymlur*'s preference for third-person narration over dialogue.

(iii) *Þrymlur and the Scandinavian Ballads*[5]

In their article on the Norwegian variant of the 'Torsvisen' ballad, Sophus Bugge and Moltke Moe identify four main strands of the Scandinavian tradition outside of Iceland (Bugge and Moe 1897, 14–15). The oldest extant version is preserved in two Danish manuscripts from the sixteenth century, NKS 815 b 4to ('Svanings Håndskrift I, 4to') (*c*.1580) and GKS 2397 4to ('Rentzells Håndskrift, Nr. 35') (*c*.1580) (University of Copenhagen n.d.), and is hereafter referred to as 'Dan. A'. A second Danish variant was collected in the nineteenth century on Jylland and is hereafter referred to as 'Dan. C'.[6] A Swedish variant (hereafter 'Sw.') was collected in Västergötland in the seventeenth century and is preserved in a manuscript from *c*.1670 (KB Vs 20) (Jonsson et al., eds, 2001, 85). Though the Norwegian variant was first collected in the 1750s, it is generally taken to represent the oldest strand of the tradition (Bugge and Moe 1897, 65; Harris 2012, 163–64).

A version of the ballad also seems to have been known on the Faroe Islands, though only fragments are known to us. These consist of two stanzas translated into Danish, contained in a letter from the pastor Johan Henrik Schrøter to Bishop Peter Erasmus Müller in the year 1820 (Grüner Nielsen 1911, 72–76).[7] These stanzas, as Schrøter reports them, are as follows:

---

[5] The ballads are cited from the following editions: The Norwegian text is taken from the University of Oslo's text, 'Torekall vinn att hamaren sin', from their Dokumentationsprojekt website. The Swedish text follows that in Jonsson et al., eds, 2001, 85–86. The Danish A-text follows that in Grundtvig, ed., 1966, 1 1–7, and the C-text is given in IV 578–83 of the same work.

[6] This title has been chosen over the more obvious 'Dan. B' following Bugge and Moe's example; they use 'Dan. B' for Vedel's 1591 edition of the text, which is largely identical to Dan. A and will not be discussed here.

[7] The letter in question is contained in the miscellany AM 972 a 4to.

1. Thore kom af Skoven hiem,
   Træt var han af Færde;
   Trold havde taget Hammeren hen,
   han vidste sig intet at giøre.

Thorer tæmmer sin fole med gode Stunder.

2. 'Hør du Loke underlige,
   Leie Tienner min:
   vil du fare til Snûde-Trolden
   og hente mig Hammeren hiem.'   (Grüner Nielsen 1911, 72)

   Thore came home from the woods,
   he was tired from his journey;
   a troll had taken his hammer,
   he didn't know what to do with himself.

Thore leads his horse a good while.

   'Listen carefully, Loki
   my servant:
   you will travel to the Snout-Troll(?)
   and bring my hammer home.'

Schrøter comments that he has translated *med gode Stunder* 'for a good while' from *uj Toûma*, which suggests that the original Faroese version had a refrain very similar to that found in the Norwegian and Swedish variants: *Thorekal tome naa Foelan sin med toumer* (Norw.) and *Thorer tämjer fåhlan sin i tömme* (Thorekal/Thorer breaks in his foal to bridle) (Sw.). Hakon Grüner Nielsen has discussed the Faroese fragments in some detail and concluded that the ballad arrived there by way of Norway, though allowing for a certain amount of influence from the Swedish branch of the tradition (Grüner Nielsen 1911, 76–78).

The ultimate origin of the Scandinavian *Torsvisen* remains a subject of debate. Sophus Bugge and Moltke Moe's 1895 publication, *Torsvisen i sin norske form*, remains the most extensive discussion of the relationships between the various ballad versions and many other texts from medieval Scandinavia and Iceland. Bugge and Moe maintain that the ballad originated in Norway and was strongly influenced by both *Þrymskviða* and *Þrymlur*, as well as potentially by Icelandic oral informants (Bugge and Moe 1897, 86, 114). They see the ballad tradition as soon diverging into two distinct branches, with the Danish variants being the product of later reworkings influenced by chivalric texts (64), and the Swedish variant, though closer to the Norwegian, also being influenced by the Danish ballads (65). This view is far from universal, however: Bengt R. Jonsson, for example, proposes that, rather than *Þrymlur* serving as a source for the ballads, it was the other way around, with Þrymlur originating later than the earliest ballad variant (Jonsson 1991, 157). Aurelijus Vijūnas, meanwhile, argues that there is no direct relationship between the ballads and the Icelandic material, and that the later texts instead derive independently from a lost 'proto-myth' version of the hammer story (Vijūnas 2019, 3). However, although it seems likely that the ballads' authors were also working with their own sources of information, the verbal correspondences discussed below do suggest some degree of interaction between their works and the Icelandic texts.

As neither Þrymlur nor the ballads were recorded before the mid-sixteenth century, however, and both Þrymlur and the 'original' Norwegian ballad have a suggested date of composition significantly predating this,[8] it is impossible to be sure in which direction influence can be said to flow. Moreover, the issue is further clouded by the fact that people familiar with one or more of the extant texts, not to mention other, unrecorded traditions surrounding the theft of Þórr's hammer, were almost certainly interacting with one another on a regular basis over the centuries.

As this section of the introduction is only intended to situate Þrymlur in its wider literary and oral context, the following is far from an exhaustive discussion of all points of difference between Þrymlur, Þrymskviða and the ballads. Instead it aims to give an overview of the most significant points of divergence at both a structural and narrative level.

In terms of structure, the most striking difference between the texts is their wildly disparate lengths. The Swedish ballad is the shortest, at only sixteen stanzas. In its extant form, the Norwegian is the next shortest at eighteen stanzas, but as it breaks off at the point where Gremmil wonders at the bride's appetite, it may be assumed that a complete version would be at least several stanzas longer. The Danish A-text is twenty-three stanzas and the C-text twenty-five. Þrymskviða comes to thirty-three stanzas, but Þrymlur is by far the longest, clocking in at seventy-nine stanzas and over twice as many words as its nearest rival. It should be noted that, compared to later examples of the *rímur* genre, Þrymlur is rather short, but even its shortest individual *ríma* is comparable to the length of the longest ballad. This would perhaps fit with the possible performance context of *rímur* discussed above; although there are no concrete sources to connect the earliest Scandinavian ballads to dance, the fact that their origins lie in French dance tunes (Colbert 1989, 131), combined with the knowledge

---

[8] Joseph Harris argues that the Norwegian ballad originated in the early fourteenth century 'when Þrymskviða was still known there as an oral poem' (Harris 2012, 163).

that in later centuries they certainly were danced to, both in Scandinavia and Iceland, strongly suggests that even the earlier ballads were performed at dances (Aðalheiður Guðmundsdóttir 2007).[9]

	Refrain	Stanzas	Lines (excl. refrain)	Words (excl. refrain)	% dialogue
Þrymskviða	No	33	265	756	46.8
Þrymlur	No	79	293	1532	25.2
Norw.	Yes	18	72	342	50.0
Sw.	Yes	16	64	307	53.1
Dan. A	Yes	23	92	490	37.0
Dan. C	Yes	25	100	545	40.0

Table 1: Structural comparison with ballads

There are several structural similarities that are shared by *Þrymskviða* and the ballads, but not by *Þrymlur*. As can be seen in Table 1, *Þrymlur* is notably low on dialogue compared to the other texts. The ballads average 45% dialogue, *Þrymskviða* 46.8%, and *Þrymlur* a mere 25.2%. This raises some interesting questions about the performance of these different genres. Terry Gunnell has argued that a high proportion of speech to narration, in Eddic poetry at least, is suggestive of dramatic performance, with multiple actors and/or costume changes to distinguish the speakers (Gunnell 1995, 186). Gunnell categorises *Þrymskviða* as 'epic-dramatic' rather than purely dramatic, the latter category being reserved for poems in *ljóðaháttr* (Gunnell 1995, 352). Whilst a semi-dramatised performance of *Þrymskviða* is certainly not impossible, and indeed the subject matter lends itself particularly well to exaggerated costume changes, the ballads' similar proportion of dialogue suggest that traditional 'theatre' should not be our only interpretation of dialogue in poetry. Theatre, in which an audience's attention is fixed on the performers, and dance, in which participants are rarely looking in the same direction for long, are not at first glance compatible forms of performance. However, as the Balladeskolen recording demonstrates (see n. 9), even in a dance context it is possible to incorporate multiple speakers—or rather, groups of speakers—and create a kind of drama in which there is no real distinction between audience and performers. The fact that, in the ballads, a change of speaker occurs only at the start of a new stanza or half-stanza would also make this kind of communal performance more manageable. To

---

[9] A modern dance performance of 'Tor af Havsgård' (the Dan. C text) can be seen at http://www.balladeskolen.dk/dgf001.htm.

a certain extent, *Þrymskviða* also employs this trick of changing speakers on the stanza/half-stanza, though not nearly as consistently as the ballads. *Þrymlur*, on the other hand, makes no such attempt, and indeed even has one line which switches from third-person narration to dialogue partway through (I.24.2). This, along with the narrator's occasional self-insertion of *frá eg* 'I have heard' or similar, argues strongly in favour of a single performer for *Þrymlur* as it was originally conceived.

A further point of similarity between the ballads and *Þrymkviða* is in their extensive use of repetition. Each of the ballads contains a refrain, as is typical of the genre, but all also echo at least one stanza with only the most minor variation. This latter technique of tying the narrative together is also employed in *Þrymskviða*. A motif which lends itself particularly well to this sort of repetition is Loki's flight to and from the giants' home. In *Þrymskviða* and the two Danish ballads, these two sets of verses are near-perfect verbal echoes of each other, with only the destination and point of departure being changed:

> Fló þá Loki
> —fjaðrhamr dunði—
> unz fyr útan kom
> **ása garða**
> ok fyr innan kom
> **jǫtna heima**.   (*Þrymskviða* 5, *Eddukvæði* I, 422)

> Fló þá Loki
> —fjaðrhamr dunði—
> unz fyr útan kom
> **jǫtna heima**
> ok fyr innan kom
> **ása garða**.   (*Þrymskviða* 9, *Eddukvæði* I, 423)

Loki flew then—the feather-form resounded—until he came outside **Ásgarðr/Jǫtunheimar** and came inside **Jǫtunheimar/Ásgarðr**.

> Thet vor liden Locke,
> setter sig i fiedder-hamme:
> saa fløg hand **till Nørre-field**
> alt offuer thet salthe vand.   (*Dan. A* 3)

> Thet vor liden Locke,
> setter sig i fedder-ham:
> saa fløg hand **till-bage igien**
> alt offuer det salte vannd.   (*Dan. A* 9)

That was little Locke, he dressed himself in a feather-shape: thus he flew **to Norrefjeld/back again** all over the salt water.

Introduction xxxi

> Mit udi den gaard
> ther axler hand sin skinnd:
> saa gick hand i stoffuen
> alt for **then thosse-greffue** ind.   (*Dan. A* 4)

> Mit udi den gaard
> der axler hand sin skind,
> saa ganger han i stuffuen
> alt for **sin broder** ind.   (*Dan. A* 10) (*DgF* I, 3–4)

Just outside the homestead, there he shrugged on his skin-cloak: thus he went into the chamber, all for **the troll-lord/his brother** inside.

> Det var Lokki Læjermand,
> satt' sig i Fjederham:
> saa sejled han **til Norgefjæld**
> over Søer og salten Vand.   (*Dan. C* 2)

> Det var Lokki Læjermand,
> satt' sig i Fjederham:
> saa sejled han **tilbag' igjen**
> over Søer og salten Vand.   (*Dan. C* 8)

That was Lokki Læjermand, he dressed himself in a feather-shape: thus he sailed **to Norgefjeld/back again** over sea and salt water.

> Det var Lokki Læjermand,
> han styred hans Snejke for Land:
> og det var den **gode Tossegrev'**,
> spaseret sig nede ved Strand. (*Dan. C* 3)

> Det var Lokki Læjermand,
> han styred hans Snejke for Land:
> og det var **Tor aa Haagensgaard**
> spaseret sig nede ved Strand. (*Dan. C* 9) (*DgF* IV, 581)

That was Lokki Læjermand, he steered his ship towards land, and there was **the good troll-lord/Tor of Haagensgaard**, promenading down the beach.

All four ballads repeat this trick when it comes to reporting Loki's conversation with the giant and his subsequent report of that conversation to Þórr. Again, this is also seen in *Þrymskviða*, though not to the same extent. Here, only four lines are echoed:

> 'Hann engi maðr
> aptr um heimtir,
> nema fœri **mér**
> Freyju at kvæn.'   (*Þrymskviða* 8) (*Eddukvæði* I, 423)

> 'Hann engi maðr
> aptr um heimtir,

nema **honum** fœri
Freyju at kván.' (*Þrymskviða* 11)
'No man will reclaim it unless you give **me/him** Freyja as a bride.'

As already discussed, *Þrymskviða* gets a great deal of mileage out of the transformation scene: Heimdallr proposes the plan in lurid detail, Þórr makes his objections known in no uncertain fashion, but the plan is carried out nonetheless, complete with all Heimdallr's suggestions. The ballads, however, do not echo this scene; though the idea of hair-brushing occurs in two successive stanzas in the Norwegian variant, it is phrased differently each time, and no phrases are repeated even to that extent in any of the other ballads.

The poet of *Þrymlur* does not employ this level of repetition at any point. The longest repeated phrase is *Nema þér Freyju færið mér* 'Unless you bring me Freyja', which appears in both Þrymr's initial ransom demand (st.I.25) and Loki's later report (st.I.28). This, along with the phrase *ýtar bjuggu Ása-Þór*, which appears twice during Þórr's makeover, is the sum total of repetition in the *rímur*. This is typical of the genre, whose practitioners demonstrate their skill through finding original ways to express repeated ideas—hence the later, extensive use of kennings (Vésteinn Ólason 1982, 53). Structurally, therefore, the ballads bear very little resemblance to *Þrymlur*, which may explain why Finnur Jónsson discounts it as a possible source for them (Finnur Jónsson 1920, 39).

Turning now to points of narrative content, it is apparent that the ballads bear a greater similarity to one another than to either Icelandic version. Though both *Þrymskviða* and *Þrymlur* explicitly identify their protagonists as Æsir, this is apparently not the case in any of the ballads. That said, the ballads clearly take place in a world where the supernatural is not out of place. The antagonists are 'trolls' or 'giants': *jutulen* (Norw.), *Trolltram* (Sw.), *tossegreve* (Dan. A and C), *små trolde* (Dan. A), and *små trollen* (Sw.). Moreover, Þórr (Torekall/Tårkar/Tor/Tord) and his assistant (Laakien/Locke Lewe/liden Locke/Lokki Læjermand) seem possessed of some more-than-mortal abilities themselves, since Loki is capable of flight in all four versions, and Þórr is able to lift the hammer with ease when the trolls struggle to shift it. This latter ability is perhaps hinted at in *Þrymlur*, where we are told that an elderly giantess, probably Þrymr's mother Syrpa, is able to carry the hammer where a hundred men have failed to move it:

   Hvergi gátu hamarinn fært
   hundrað manns, þó til sé hrært.
   Keila setti upp kryppu bein,
   kerling gat þó borið hann ein. (*Þrymlur* III.21)

> By no means could the hammer be moved
> though a hundred men attempt to shift it.
> Keila raised her bony hump,
> yet the old woman could carry it on her own.

Similar verses appear in all the ballads, except the Norwegian one, which breaks off before this point:

> Fembtan wore dhe små trollen,
> som buhre dän hammaren ihn
> Bruden tahr honom med ena hand
> och sticker honom Vnder sit skind. (*Sw.* 15) (*SMB* 5:1, 86)

> Fifteen were the small trolls
> who bore the hammer in.
> The bride takes it with a single hand
> and sticks it under her skin.[10]

> Otte vor di kiemper,
> der hammeren bar ind paa træ:
> det vill ieg for sandinen sige:
> di lagde hannem offuer brudens knæ. (*Dan. A* 20)

> Eight were those champions
> who bore the hammer in on a tray:
> that I will truthfully say:
> they laid it across the bride's knee.

> Thet vor da den unge brud,
> tog hammeren i sin haand:
> det vill ieg for sandingen sige:
> hun slønget hannem som en vand. (*Dan. A* 21) (*DgF* I, 4)

> It was then the young bride
> who took the hammer in her hand:
> that I will truthfully say:
> she threw it like a wand.

> Tolv saa vare de Kæmper
> den Hammer kast' op af Jord:
> men atten saa vare de Kæmper
> den Hammer bar ind på Bord. (*Dan. C* 22)

> So twelve were the champions
> who threw the hammer up from the ground,
> but eighteen were the champions
> who bore the hammer to the table.

---

[10] Presumably some sort of garment or lap-covering.

> Atten saa vare de Kæmper
> den Hammer bar ind paa Bord:
> men det var goden unge Brud,
> [hun] tog den i Fingre to.   (*Dan.* C 23) (*DgF* IV, 582)
>
> So eighteen were the champions
> who bore the hammer to the table,
> but it was the good young bride
> who took it in two fingers.

Whether this is a special power of the hammer—a possible Excaliburesque motif in which the hammer may only be wielded by the worthy—or a comment on the bride's superhuman strength, the fact remains that this motif does not appear in *Þrymskviða* in any form. In *Þrymskviða*, the disappearance and subsequent return of the hammer both occur 'off-stage': Þrymr gives the order for the hammer to be fetched and the next stanza reveals Þórr's joy at the reunion, but no narrative space is devoted to the process of actually retrieving the hammer, suggesting that the poet did not see this as being in any way difficult. This absence is one point in favour of *Þrymlur* as an additional source for the ballads.

Another point in *Þrymlur*'s favour as a source is its portrayal of Loki as a servant or slave of the Æsir. This is hinted at in *Þrymskviða*, where it is certainly Loki who does all the actual work in the story and who accompanies Þórr to Jǫtunheimar disguised as his *ambátt* 'maid', but the Loki of *Þrymskviða* is not so subservient that he has any hesitation in telling Þórr to shut up when the situation calls for it. In *Þrymlur*, however, Loki is explicitly called *Fjölnis þjón* 'Fjǫlnir's servant' and *Óðins þræl* 'Óðinn's slave' (st. I.21), and this idea also appears in the Swedish ballad, where Locke is addressed as *legedrängen min* 'my hired servant', though in the Danish branch of the tradition he is Tor/Tord's brother.

This variation no doubt reflects the ambiguous role Loki plays in almost all the early texts concerning him. *Snorra Edda* refers to him as *rógbera Ásanna* 'slanderer of the Æsir' and *vǫmm allra goða ok manna* 'the shame of all gods and men', but also as *sinna ok sessa Óðins ok Ása* 'companion and benchmate of Óðinn and the Æsir' (Faulkes, ed., 2005, 26; Faulkes, ed., 2007, 20). Many of the tales related in *Snorra Edda* feature Loki initially causing problems for the gods (e.g. by stealing Sif's hair, kidnapping Iðunn, agreeing to the Master-Builder's bargain) but in the end, improving their standing (e.g. the dwarves who craft new hair for Sif also create many of the treasures the Æsir are later known for; by tricking the Master-Builder, the Æsir get an impregnable wall for free). The *Poetic Edda* reflects similar ambiguities. For instance, *Vǫluspá* depicts Loki as a captive of the Æsir, but in *Lokasenna,* a poem in which Loki goes out of his way to insult the gods, he reminds Óðinn that they used to be blood-brothers: *Vit í árdaga / blendum blóði saman* 'We, in the olden days, mixed our blood together' and presents himself as the lover of a number of the Ásynjur, charges which none of them deny (*Eddukvæði,* 299–300; 410).

Another commonality between *Þrymlur* and the ballads is their poets' shared enjoyment of the grotesque. Whilst this is seen to some extent in *Þrymskviða* too, the *rímur* and ballads all go the extra mile. As already discussed, this is particularly noticeable in the texts' violent conclusions, but it is also apparent at the wedding feast. In *Þrymskviða* the bride eats oxen, eight salmon, unspecified delicacies and three measures of mead. In *Þrymlur,* the number of salmon has increased to twelve. In the Norwegian ballad, she eats two pounds of oxen, all the bread available, fifteen bushels of grain, fifty salmon, plus plenty of small fish, just for good measure. In the Danish A-text, she eats a whole ox, fifteen hams and seven hundred loaves of bread. In the C-text, the oxen reappear, along with fat sheep and seven hams. In the C-text, this scene is given full comic rein, extending over five stanzas during which the 'bride' declares:

> 'Eder a lidt, aa eder a møj',
> aalder fór a nok:
> før a fór edt mi Brujgrød,
> der er lavet i en Syvtønd'-Pott'. (*Dan. C* 20)

> I'll eat a little and eat a lot
> and never get enough,
> before I get to eat my wedding-porridge,
> which is made in a seven-tun pot.

> Eder a lidt aa eder a møj',
> aalder blyvver a mæt:
> før a fór mi Bro'ers Hammer aa séj,
> som saa læng' har været forgjæt.' (*Dan. C* 21) (*DgF* IV, 582)

> I'll eat a little and eat a lot,
> and never become satisfied,
> before I get to see my brother's hammer,
> which has so long been forgotten.

The Swedish ballad does not contain an overeating scene, but given its abrupt jumps in narrative, not to mention the general sparseness of its account, it seems likely that the extant text is incomplete.

The ballads outstrip even *Þrymlur* in their Freyja character's reaction to the news of her impending marriage. In *Þrymksviða,* she is certainly angry—she snorts so loudly that the halls shake and Brisingamen bursts—

and in Þrymlur she declares that she will throw herself into the sea rather than marry a giant. Yet the Norwegian and Swedish ballads are even more melodramatic, bordering on the grotesque. In the Norwegian version, *Hun drev bloet af aa len sin /Hun svartna ret som ai Joele* 'She drove the blood from her face. She became black just like the earth' (st. 11), and in the Swedish, *hoon blef så illa widh / Däth sprack af hwar finger bloden vth / och ran på Jorden nidh* 'she took this so badly that the blood sprang out from each finger and ran onto the earth below' (st. 8). In the Danish A-text, however, she simply states that she would rather marry a Christian man than a troll.

Freyja's reaction here helps to set the scene for the subsequent cross-dressing plot. In both Icelandic texts, her refusal prompts the rest of the gods to hold a council, during which Heimdallr proposes Þórr's disguise. In the Norwegian ballad, no one directly proposes the scheme; the stanza after the sister's refusal simply begins with an unspecified 'they' arraying the bride in her wedding garments—and moreover, it is nowhere stated that this bride is in fact Torekall, as this version of the ballad breaks off before any dramatic revelation can take place. The Swedish ballad contains an interesting verse in which Tårkar asks Frojenborg how much she will pay him to go as the bride in her stead; she makes no reply, but in the next stanza we are told that *Thet war Tårkar sielfwer . . . där han skulle brud wara* 'That was Tårkar himself . . . he shall be the bride' (st. 10). This request for money is not found in any of the other ballads, but it does have a possible parallel in Þrymlur. Here, when Þórr informs Freyja of Þrymr's demands, she tells him, '*Þigg nú málm og menið hið góða*' 'Now receive metal (i.e. gold, jewellery) and the good necklace' (II.3). This is long before the cross-dressing scheme is proposed, so she is clearly not offering jewels to help with his disguise; the most likely explanation is that these represent the same bribery motif as is seen in the Swedish ballad. The Danish ballads introduce the character of the 'old father', who is usually identified with the Þórr figure although this is nowhere stated explicitly—indeed, the C-text, which concludes *saa lakked hun hjem til Tor* 'thus she wandered home to Tor' (st. 25), seems to imply that Tor was not a part of the wedding party. In the A-text, an unidentified speaker, possibly Lokke, proposes that they take *vor gamle fader* 'our old father' (st. 13), brush his hair and array him in bridal finery, before sending him off to be wed. In the C-text, Tor's sister does not even have time to react to the proposed wedding before *Op stod djer gammel Oldefaa'r* 'up stood the old great-grandpa' (st. 12) who willingly volunteers for the part. The variation contained in this single scene significantly affects how we view each ballad variant as a text, as well as our impressions of the characters in each: a Tårkar who is willing enough to be dressed as a bride as long as he's paid for the job is very different from the Þórr who is so concerned about being called *argr*, who is in turn very different from the old man who cheerfully volunteers for the role and later informs the trolls that he's not going anywhere until he's had his porridge.

Whilst the ballads and *Þrymlur* tend to play up the broadly humorous aspects of the story, when compared to *Þrymskviða*, they also downplay one of the few serious aspects of the poem: the idea that Þórr's hammer is in the hands of his enemies. In *Þrymskviða*, the gravity of the situation is brought home by Loki's reminder in stanza 18 that giants will soon have occupied Ásgarðr unless the hammer is retrieved. The dire necessity of retrieving the hammer is never stated in any of the other poems, and indeed *Þrymlur*'s emphasis on Þórr's emotions—sorrow and distress at its loss, joy at its return—suggests that, as far as the other gods are concerned, the main motive for finding the hammer is to rid themselves of a sulky Þórr. This lowering of the stakes is neatly symbolised by the respective depths at which the hammer is buried. In *Þrymskviða*, Þrymr informs Loki that it lies *átta rǫstum fyr jǫrð neðan* 'eight leagues below the earth'. In the Swedish and Danish A-text, this distance has shrunk to *femton famnar och fyratio* / *femten favne og fyrretyve* 'fifteen and forty fathoms', *fire og fyrretyv favn* 'four and forty fathoms' in the Danish C-text, a mere *åtte alni* 'eight ells' in the Norwegian ballad, and an underwhelming *níu feta* 'nine feet' in *Þrymlur*—this last particularly unimpressive in light of the fact that Þórr is here described as being twenty ells high himself.

On an even finer level of detail, there are a number of words and phrases that occur in more than one of the texts. Bugge and Moe (1897) discuss these verbal parallels more extensively than is possible here; the following is only an overview of the more readily apparent examples. Perhaps the most significant is the use of the term *fjaðrhamr* 'feather-form', which appears in both of the Icelandic poems, but is not found in the Norwegian ballad, generally considered to be closest to the ballad's original form (Harris 2012, 163). It resurfaces in the two Danish versions, which leads Bugge and Moe to conclude that the composer of at least the earlier text was independently familiar with the Icelandic material as well as the Norwegian ballad (Bugge and Moe 1897, 86). However, the Danish versions differ from the Icelandic texts in that the *fjaðrhamr* here seems to belong to their Loki figure, rather than Freyja—an understanding parallel to that of the Norwegian and Swedish versions, in which Loki has his own power of flight. The term also appears elsewhere in the Danish ballad corpus, meaning that the Torsvisen poets could have encountered it without direct recourse to the Icelandic material.[11]

A further recurrent phrase is *breiða steina*, with which Þórr is adorned during his transformation. This precise phrase is used in both *Þrymskviða*: *en á brjósti / breiða steina* 'and on his breast, broad (gem)stones' (sts 16, 19) and *Þrymlur*: *settu á bringu breiða steina* 'set on his breast broad (gem)stones' (II.9), and is perhaps echoed in the Danish C-text. Here, the stanza goes: *Så blev der silke og hvide sandal / alt på den sorte jord bred* 'So there was silk and white sendal, all on the broad black earth' (st. 14). These lines appear to be a conflation of several elements found in other versions: *Þrymlur* II.9 connects 'broad stones' and 'pure silk', whilst the Norwegian st. 11 says that Torekall's sister 'becomes black as earth', suggesting that 'black' is a formulaic descriptor in this context, one that could easily become attached to the separate idea of 'broad stones/earth' in a poet's mind.

Finally, there is the *Søer og salten Vand* 'lakes and salt water' (st. 2) over which Lokki flies in the Danish C-Text. Bugge and Moe connect this to the way in which Loki travels to Jötunheimar *einn veg lögu sem geima* 'water in the same way as sea' (st. I.20) in *Þrymlur*, but *lögr* is by no means as specific as *søer*, meaning simply 'water', or even 'liquid' in its vaguest sense. Overall, the evidence is suggestive but probably insufficient to prove Bugge and Moe's theory that the Danish ballads have an independent link to the Icelandic material.

(v) *Conclusion*

Þrymskviða draws on many motifs found across the Baltic region and beyond, bringing them together in a poem which combines lively humour with infectious rhythm. It is therefore not surprising that this tale of 'how Þórr won back his hammer' should have proved so popular across Scandinavia, from the medieval period to the present. *Þrymlur* is merely one example of how poets through the ages reworked this material to suit their own purposes.

We are unlikely ever to know for sure what those purposes were, but several possible motives for the creation of *Þrymlur* spring to mind. In an article on *Þrymskviða*, John McKinnell has argued that poetry about mythological figures could have maintained a social function even in the

---

[11] As an example, the term is used repeatedly in 'Germand Gladensvend' (Ballad no. 33 in *DgF* 2, 1–13), found in Karen Brahe E I, 1 ('Karen Brahes Folio'), *c*.1583 (University of Copenhagen n.d.).

post-Conversion period by playing a secular role as a form of therapy-through-catharsis for its listeners (McKinnell 2014, 200–20). This can also be said of *Þrymlur*, although here the audience's anxieties seem to have taken the form of questions of practical strength rather than concerns about unstable gender categories. The distancing effect achieved by projecting social concerns onto mythological figures in fact works better at the time of *Þrymlur*'s composition, precisely because of the audience's unfamiliarity, and therefore less close identification, with the figures of Þórr and Loki.

However, we should also not neglect what John D. Niles has termed the 'ludic function' of oral performance: the idea that people in all times and places have sought to be entertained (Niles 1999, 70). Although the precise performance context of early *rímur* is uncertain, their emphasis on rhyme and rhythm do argue in favour of recital as part of a dance, at least on some occasions. Many of the changes made in the telling of *Þrymlur* suggest a poet making life easier for an audience who, in the first place, were probably not completely familiar with the mythological material, and in the second, may have had their minds on other activities. Moreover, these stories are *fun*. Judging by the number of Eddic poems and tales in *Snorra Edda* about the gods bickering among themselves, this is a pattern that has been enjoyed for centuries; notably, *Lokrur*, the only other *rímur* about the gods, also revolves around Loki and Þórr's buddy-cop dynamic. In the ballads, whose popular reception was such that variants of them are still performed to this day, the comic aspects are given full rein, the material is distilled down to its most entertaining points.

That said, *Þrymlur* seems designed to convey information as well as to entertain, and therefore occupies a unique position amongst the extant poetry concerned with the theft of Þórr's hammer. *Þrymskviða*, assuming its audience's knowledge of the characters, sees no need to educate that audience. The ballads remove events from the mythological sphere entirely. Torekall and Laakien exist only within the confines of the ballad; there is no wider mythological world to relate them to, and the audience therefore does not need to be informed of any background. *Þrymlur*, in contrast, occupies a medial position between these two extremes: the mythological world is not inhabited to such a degree as to make explanation unnecessary, but nor is it abandoned. The *rímur* poet seems to target an audience on the edge of forgetting; by including the lists of giant names alongside colourful scenes of the giants' (lack of) table manners, the poet both entertains the audience and shores up collective memory of the mythological world.

8. Previous editions

Þrymlur was edited for the first time by Theodor Möbius in his *Edda Sæmundar hins fróða* (1860). The cycle appears in this edition in normalised spelling (Möbius 1860, 235–39) along with *Völsungs rímur* (240–54) and a limited number of textual notes (301). The edition is marred by some errors and imprecision, but it can be lauded as an early attempt to make *rímur* texts available to a larger scholarly community. The printing of *Þrymskviða* and *Þrymlur* within the same volume facilitates comparison.

The next edition of *Þrymlur* was by Finnur Jónsson, who in 1896 edited *Fernir forníslenzkir rímnaflokkar*, which printed *Lokrur*, *Þrymlur*, *Griplur* and *Völsungs rímur* with a short introduction focused on linguistic matters. The text is normalised and its accuracy is an improvement on the edition by Möbius. Many emendations are made, and the stanzas are rearranged in a more logical order.

Finnur Jónsson edited *Þrymlur* again in the first volume of his *Rímnasafn* (1905–12). Most of the emendations from the previous edition are repeated but the stanzas are rearranged somewhat differently. The text is diplomatic. We have noticed one unfortunate error (<fai> for <faer> in I.28.4) and two minor ones (<Kappenn> for <Kappen> in I.8.1 and <Vgxa> for <Wgxa> in III.10.1).

Although not a stand-alone edition, Jón Helgason's 1975 article 'Noter til Þrymlur' contains a wealth of textual notes which we have made use of.

The debt this edition owes to previous editors should be obvious, and we resort to many of the same emendations as Finnur Jónsson in order to make sense of difficult stanzas. The present edition is, however, somewhat closer to the text of the manuscript, and we have left the order of the stanzas as it is in the only witness. The preserved order is probably the result of confusion in the transmission, but there is no single clear way to fix it and it is the sort of difficulty which readers can profitably engage with on their own.

9. About this edition

For each stanza we provide the following:

(a) A diplomatic transcript of the text of AM 604 g 4to.

(b) A text in normalised spelling, intended to represent more or less the state of the poet's language. The normalisation is similar to that in Finnur Jónsson's *Ordbog til rímur*, but ours reflects a slightly earlier state. One difference from Finnur's norm is that we have opted to render old *vá* as such, in accordance with the poet's rhyming practices. Furthermore, we have not simplified morphological double consonants in stressed syllables, even after long vowels, in forms like *Þórr*. We have opted for *ft* rather than *pt* in words like *oft*, in accordance with the practices of the *Dictionary of Old Norse Prose* (*ONP*). In words like *Loftr/Loftur* we include epenthetic *u* in the normalised text where the metre demands it, but leave it out elsewhere as well as in the English translation and the glossary.

(c) The normalised text includes such emendations as we have deemed necessary, marked with asterisks. There is no clear line between emendation and normalisation of sloppy or unusual spelling. We have tended to mark even marginal cases with an asterisk.

(d) Each stanza has a translation into English prose, aiming at clarity and accuracy.

(e) Most stanzas have accompanying notes, which aim to explain our emendations, clarify, (or at least point out) points of ambiguity in the text, and provide referenes to similar or related texts where appropriate. As these notes are often editorial in nature, they refer to the diplomatic transcription rather than the normalised text.

There is a glossary at the back of this volume which, in addition to giving definitions of individual words, also explains the kennings used in *Þrymlur*, and provides a list of the various names used interchangeably by the poet to refer to their characters. All headwords are given in their normalised forms.

ÞRYMLUR

I

Stanza I.1

. . . ok enn frægi ullur.	. . . og enn frægi Ullr
er feingu brader hrafnne.	er fengu bráðir hrafni.
loke er sagdur lymsku fullur.	Loki er sagður lymskufullr
enn loptur odru nafnne.	en Loftur öðru nafni.

Translation: . . . and the famous Ullr, who gave flesh to the raven. Loki is said to be full of cunning, and Loftr by another name.

Notes: [1] The stanza is defective, the previous leaf being lost from the manuscript. There is no copy predating the loss. — [2] <feingu>: The verb is in the plural, indicating that Ullr alone is not the subject. Presumably another god was mentioned in the lost part of line 1. Finnur Jónsson (*Rs* I, 278) suggests the missing part was *Forseti* but this would leave us with an unmetrical line. Bugge and Moe (1897, 83) suggest the missing part was *Freyr var þar*, which has the advantage of being metrical. — [2] <brader hrafnne>: This collocation occurs in several *rímur*. The closest parallel is in *Vilmundar rímur* I.19: *Þesse er kiænn vid kilfings rendur / ad kliufa brädir hrafne / því var Hiarande af hóldum kiendur / huida odru nafne* (Ólafur Halldórsson 1975, 35). — [3] <loke>: The word <loke> is written again above the word apparently in the same hand; presumably because the first letters are a little smudged. — [4] <loptur>: The name *Loftr* for Loki also occurs in *Lokrur*, in *Snorra Edda* and in skaldic poetry.

Stanza I.2

Fenris ulfen frænde hans.	*Fenrisúlfrinn frændi hans,
frægur er hann af gleipnne.	frægr er hann af Gleipni,
margur hefur þat mællt til sanns.	margur hefur það mælt til sanns
at moder se hann at sleipne.	að móðir sé hann að Sleipni.

Translation: His kinsman, the Fenris-wolf, is famous for [how he dealt with] Gleipnir. Many have truthfully said that he [Loki] is the mother of Sleipnir.

Notes: [All] The story of the Fenris-wolf and the chain Gleipnir is found in *Gylfaginning* and in *Litla-Skálda* but only *Gylfaginning* mentions the wolf's concern with the fame he may or not gain from it. The story of Loki's impregnation with Sleipnir is found in *Gylfaginning* (Faulkes, ed., 2005, 34–35) and alluded to in *Hyndluljóð* (st. 41, *Eddukvæði*, 467).

— [1] <ulfen>: Since this is accusative but the following word is in the nominative there seems to be no way to parse the text as preserved. We follow Möbius and Finnur Jónsson in emending to the nominative form. — [4] <hann>: This must refer to Loki, which is awkward since the previous <hann> in line 2 refers to the Fenris-wolf. Jón Helgason (1975, 244) suggests that lines 3–4 originally came before lines 1–2.

Stanza I.3

Eige kom þat odni uel.	Eigi kom það Óðni vel,
ok efldu storra pretta.	og efldu *stóra pretta;
dotter loka mun heit hel.	dóttir Loka mun *heita Hel;
harka born eru þetta.	harka-börn eru þetta.

Translation: This did not suit Óðinn well—and they performed great deceits. Loki's daughter is called Hel. These are rough children.

Notes: [2] <ok>: Finnur Jónsson emends this word to *at*, but this seems undermotivated. — [2] <efldu>: Jón Helgason (1975, 244) suggests that the second half of this stanza should be placed before its first half. Then the plural in *efldu* applies to Loki's children. — [2] <storra>: There seems to be no way to parse this line as preserved; *efla* never governs the genitive. We follow Finnur Jónsson in emending to *stóra*. In the scribe's language, the accusative plural of *prettr* was presumably *pretti*, the only form found in modern Icelandic. This might have led him to construe *pretta* as genitive and add a corresponding *r* to the preceding word. — [3] <heit>: The line as preserved is metrically and semantically defective. Möbius and Finnur Jónsson emend to *heitin*, which is possible, but *heita* seems more natural, especially when compared with *Lokrur* III.16 *Logi mun heita lítill sveinn* (*Rs*, I 303).

Stanza I.4

Loke er sagdur langur ok mior.	Loki er sagður langr og mjór
ok leik þo flest med slægdum.	og *lék þó flest með slægðum,
odensson uar asa þor.	Óðins son var Ása-Þórr,
efldur storum frægdum.	efldur stórum frægðum.

Translation: Loki is said to be tall and thin and yet tricked most with slyness. Ása-Þórr was Óðinn's son, strengthened with great fame.

Notes: [2] <leik>: We follow Möbius and Finnur Jónsson in understanding <leik> as an error or unusual spelling for *lék*. The option of emending to present tense *leikur* is not metrically attractive.

Translation: He [Þórr] has girdles, as was told to me, and there are more valuable possessions. When he girds himself with them, he is mightier than trolls.

Notes: [1] <sem greintt uar mier>: This is a phrase occurring in a number of medieval *rímur*. It should not be taken as an indication of oral sources. — [3] <spener>: Like Möbius and Finnur Jónsson we take this to be a sloppy spelling of *spennir*.

Stanza I.10

Wndra digur er òrua þundur.
ecki blidur j male.
glofa atte grines kundur
giorder uorv af stale.

Undra-digr er örva Þundr,
ekki blíðr í máli,
glófa átti *Grímnis kundr
gjörðir vóru af stáli.

Translation: The Þundr of arrows [Þórr] is marvellously stout, by no means soft in speech. Grímnir's son [Þórr] had gloves; they were made of steel.

Notes: [1] <òrua þundur>: This is a common kenning for 'man' occurring in several *rímur*, including *Lokrur*. —[3] <grines>: We follow Möbius and Finnur Jónsson in emending this senseless form to *Grímnis*.

Stanza I.11

Glofar uinna gorpum mein.
greypter hauka folldu.
hrifur hann med þeim hardan stein.
sem hendur uæri j molldu.

Glófar vinna görpum mein,
greyptir hauka foldu.
Hrífr hann með þeim harðan stein
sem hendur væri í moldu.

Translation: The gloves, covering the land of the hawks [hands], do harm to bold men. With them he grips a hard stone as if his hands were in soil.

Notes: [2] <greypter>: We follow Finnur Jónsson (*Rs*, I 288; 1926–28, 145) in understanding the word in this context to mean 'enclosing'. More typically the word means 'inlaid', usually referring to gold or steel.

Stanza I.12

Heim bod ueitte haluren stor.
hollda sueit med sigre.
sa het þrymur er þangat for.
þussa gramurenn digre.

Heimboð veitti halrinn stórr
hölda sveit með sigri,
sá hét Þrymr er þangað fór
þursa gramrinn digri.

Translation: The big man [Þórr], victorious, offered an invitation to the troop of men. Þrymr was the name of the one who travelled there, the stout lord of the giants.

Notes: [1] <stor>: We take this to agree with *halrinn* and hence normalise to *stórr* which suggests a young rhyme. Alternatively, the word could agree with (plural) *heimboð*, in which case the normalised spelling would be *stór*. See section 4 of the introduction. — [2] <med sigre>: Perhaps the intended meaning is that this was a feast in celebration of some victory or other.

Stanza I.13

Brogdin taka at birtazt stor.	Brögðin taka að birtast stór
er bragnar wor j suefne.	er bragnar *vóru í svefni,
hamarin miollner huarf fra þor.	hamarinn Mjöllnir hvarf frá Þór.
her eru brogd j efne.	Hér eru brögð í efni.

Translation: Great deceptions began to appear when the men were asleep; the hammer Mjöllnir disappeared from Þórr. Here tricks are in the offing.

Notes: [1] <taka> (written <tᶜa>) is somewhat unclear. — [1] <birtazt>: possibly corrected from <byrtazt>. — [2] <er>: Added later above the line but in the same hand. — [2] <wor>: Like Möbius and Finnur Jónsson, we take this to be an unusual spelling of *vóru*. By omitting the final vowel the scribe may be representing the elision of an unstressed vowel before an unstressed vowel-initial word. This was normal in medieval *rímur* (Haukur Þorgeirsson 2013, 111–12), but it is not normally represented in the spelling.

Stanza I.14

Huergi feingu hamre nad	Hvergi fengu hamri náð
huar sem ytar forv.	hvar sem ýtar fóru.
eingi hitter jotnna lad.	Engi hittir jötna láð.
aller þrotnner uorv.	Allir þrotnir vóru.

Translation: Nowhere could they find the hammer, wherever the men went. No one finds their way to the land of the giants. They were all exhausted.

Stanza I.15

Wpp j fagran freyiu gard.	Upp í fagran Freyju garð
fyst nam þor at ganga.	fyrst nam Þórr að ganga.
seger hann huad at sorgum uard.	Segir hann hvað að sorgum varð
ok sina mædi stranga.	og sína mæði stranga.

Translation: First Þórr headed up to Freyja's fair enclosure. He says what his sorrow was and his painful sadness.

Notes: [3] The line is metrically defective; the trochee <huad at> has a light first syllable. — [3] <sorgum>: The <r> looks as if it may have been corrected.

Stanza I.16

Freyia lia mier fiadur ham þinn	'Freyja, ljá mér fjaðrham þinn!
fliuga villde eg lata.	Fljúga vildi eg láta,
henta aptur hamarenn min	henta aftur hamarinn minn.'
hon tok sartt at grate.	Hon tók sárt að *gráta.

Translation: 'Freyja, lend me your feather-form! I want to make it fly to reclaim my hammer.' She began to cry bitterly.

Notes: [4] <hon>: The context and the structure of the stanza make it tempting to emend to *hann*. The preceding stanza emphasises Þórr's distress and the following stanza describes Freyja as happy. Also note that stanza II.18 describes Þórr (admittedly falsely) as sobbing. — [4] <grate>: Like Möbius and Finnur Jónsson, we see no alternative to emending to *gráta*, fixing both the sense and the rhyme.

Stanza I.17

Fiadur ham tacktu furdu bratt.	'Fjaðrham taktu furðu brátt,'
fliodit talar hit teita.	fljóðið talar hið teita.
ef þu hamarinn hitta matt.	'Ef þú hamarinn hitta mátt,
huer skal epter leita.	hverr skal eftir leita?'

Translation: 'Take the feather-form very quickly,' the cheerful lady says. 'If you are to find your hammer, who shall search for it?'

Stanza I.18

Loki er jafnan leitum uanur.	'Loki er jafnan leitum vanr.
leikur hann þratt um beima.	Leikr hann þrátt um beima.
hann skal skal fara sem fugllinn suanur.	Hann *skal fara sem fuglinn svanr
ok fliuga j under heima.	og fljúga í undirheima.'

Translation: 'Loki is always accustomed to searching. He frequently tricks men. He shall travel as the swan-bird and fly into the underworld.'

Notes: [1–4] It is unclear whether this stanza ought to be taken as third-person narration or as Þórr's reply to Freyja. Given the future tense of *skal fara* here, when the narration uses only the present or preterite elsewhere, direct speech seems to us to be the more plausible interpretation. — [2] Like Finnur Jónsson (1926–28, 236) we take *leika um* to mean 'trick', although, as Jón Helgason (1975, 247) points out, this sense is not otherwise attested (the expected phrase would be *leika á*). Jón suggests instead that *beima* is a corruption of *geima* and that the line referred to Loki flying over the sea. — [4] <under heima>: The word occurs in some late medieval romances but not in other mythological sources.

Stanza I.19

Gumnum þotti granda fæst.	Gumnum þótti granda fæst
garpnum bragda drivga.	garpnum bragða drjúga.
fiadurham hafdi loptur læst.	Fjaðrham hafði Loftur læst.
loke tok hatt at fliuga.	Loki tók hátt að fljúga.

Translation: People thought few things would hurt the man full of tricks. Loftr had locked the feather-form [onto his body?]. Loki began to fly high.

Stanza I.20

Flygur hann ut yfer ása gard.	Flýgr hann út yfir ása garð
ein ueg logu sem geima.	einn veg *lönd sem geima.
karlli jllt j kryppu uard.	Karli illt í kryppu varð.
hann kemur j jotnna heima.	Hann kemr í jötna heima.

Translation: He flies out over Ásgarðr the same way over land as sea. He felt pain in his hunched back. He comes into the giants' world.

Notes: [2] <logu sem geima>: This is a thorny problem. Bugge and Moe (1897, 75–76) note that one Danish version of the ballad has *over søer og salten vand* 'over lakes and salt water' in the corresponding place and take the *Þrymlur* line to mean the same thing. But *lögr* is a much more general word than *sø* and does not refer specifically to lakes or fresh water. It seems more likely that our text has mixed up different formulaic ways of saying land and sea—expressions such as *lögu og lönd* (*Konráðs rímur* II.4, *RR*, 103) and *lönd og geima*. We have found the latter expression in some form in seven late medieval sources (*Ólafs ríma Haraldssonar* 64, *Rs*, I 8; *Sigurðar rímur þögla* I.27, Þorvaldur Sigurðsson 1986; *Sturlaugs rímur* V.4, *Rs*, II 490; *Boðorðadiktur* 82.4, AM 721 4to, 4v; *Gimsteinn* 28, 113 *ÍM* I:311, 329; *Ljómur* 32.5, *ÍM* I:136; *Ektors rímur* X.19; *Kollsbók*, 76v). Finnur Jónsson emends <logu> to *láð* which amounts to the same thing, but *láð og geima* is a rarer expression: we have found it only in *Amicus rímur* II.13 (Kölbing 1884, 193). Jón Helgason (1975, 248) half-heartedly defends the tautological *lögu sem geima* by pointing to another tautology in stanza II.15.

Stanza I.21

Fiolnes þion kom furdu dæll.	Fjölnis þjón kom furðu *dæl,
fram at landi bavgi.	fram at *landa baugi,

| ute stod fyrer odens þræll. | úti stóð fyrir Óðins *þræl |
| jotuns þrymur á haugi. | *jötunninn Þrymr á haugi. |

Translation: Fjölnir's servant [Loki] came very easily forward to the ring of lands. In front of Óðinn's thrall [Loki], the giant Þrymr stood outside on a mound.

Notes: [1] <Fiolnes>: The <s>, which has an unusual shape, is written above the line. *Fjölnir* is given as a name of Óðinn in *Gylfaginning* (Faulkes, ed., 2005, 8) and in *Óðins nǫfn* (Gurevich, ed., 2017b, 735).— [1] <þion>: Despite the single <n>, this must be a nominative form (cf. Aðalsteinn Hákonarson 2016, 99). The idea of Loki as a servant of the Æsir seems to be a late-medieval development. It also appears in st. I.5 of *Lokrur* (Finnur Jónsson, ed., 1905–12, I, 291) and in the Danish C ballad tradition, where Lokke is referred to as Tor's *legodrängen* 'hired servant'. In *Lokrur* in particular, Loki's role seems to have been combined with that of Þjálfi, with Loki preparing Þórr's goats for the evening meal (Gras 1931, 42–49). — [1] <dæll>: We emend to *dæl* on the evidence of the rhyme, assuming that it is a nominative form analogous to the preceding *þjón* and to *þrælinn* in stanza III.2. — [2] <landi>: We see no way to parse this line as preserved and follow Möbius and Finnur Jónsson in emending to *landa*. This yields *landa baugr* which is syntactically clear but semantically obscure in this context. Normally it would be a kenning referring either to the sea or to the Miðgarðsormr, but neither seems a good fit here. Finnur Jónsson (1926–28, 16) takes it to refer to the sea. — [3] <þræll>: A nominative form does not make sense here so we follow the previous editors in emending to the dative form. Jón Helgason (1975, 248) tries to make sense of the nominative and suggests emending Óðins to *aldinn*. His interpretation would entail reading *fyrir* not as a preposition but as a stressed adverb. That would, however, leave the line metrically defective. — [4] <jotuns>: This genitive form is metrically deficient and senseless in this context. We follow Finnur Jónsson in emending to *jötunninn*, assuming that an *i* with a macron was misread as a tall *s*. Möbius emends to *jötunn*, but this is less paleographically plausible and fails to fix the metrical error.

Stanza I.22

Liotur talar j lynde veill.	Ljótur talar í lyndi veill,
leidadj ordum slettum.	leiðaði orðum sléttum:
lodur kom þu hingat heill.	'Lóður, kom þú hingað heill!
huad hefur karll j frettum.	Hvað hefur karl í fréttum?'

Translation: The ugly one talks, with deceit in mind. He spoke with smooth words: 'Lóður, be welcome! What's going on, old man?'

Notes: [1] <veill>: The word usually means 'diseased', but Finnur Jónsson (1926–28, 388) takes it to mean 'deceitful' here. Jón Helgason (1975, 248) adds some arguments in support. — [2] <leidadj>: This is a problematic form. A <j> at the end of a word is atypical, but it is clearly not an <r> even though Möbius reads it as such. Furthermore, the past tense of *leiða* is normally *leiddi* rather than *leiðaði*, and we know of no instance where *leiða* is used with *orð*. The general sense must be 'spoke' but the precise shade of meaning is unclear. Jón Helgason (1975, 248) suggests a connection with *útliða* or *útleiða* which means 'to explain'. — [2] <ordum slettum>: The adjective *sléttr* is also used with *orð* in *Geirarðs rímur* I.1 (*Rs*, II 474) and *Völsungs rímur* I.3 (*Rs*, I 311).

Stanza I.23

Seger hann allt sem frettinn for.	Segir hann allt sem fréttin fór,
fyst tok loke at jnna.	fyrst tók Loki at inna:
hamarinn miollner huarf fra þor.	'hamarinn Mjöllnir hvarf frá Þór
ok huergi megum hann finna.	og hvergi megum hann finna.'

Translation: He tells him all that has happened. Loki began to explain: 'The hammer Mjöllnir disappeared from Þórr and we can't find it anywhere.'

Stanza I.24

Driug miog eru þar dulder til sanz.	'Drjúgmjög *eruð þar duldir til sanns,'
dofri talar af galldri	Dofri talar, 'af galdri
ek hefe folgit hamarinn hans.	eg hefi fólgið hamarinn hans.
hann mun finnazt alldri.	Hann mun finnast aldri,

Translation: 'In truth, you are very much deluded,' Dofri [Þrymr] says. 'By magic I have hidden his hammer; it will never be found,

Notes: [1] <eru þar>: The third person form is awkward here and Finnur emends to *eru þér*. We emend to *eruð þar* which amounts to the same thing but seems a lesser change. — [2] It is fairly common in *rímur* to substitute the name of one being for that of another from the same broad group. For example, a number of *rímur* refer to the mead of poetry as some kind of liquid belonging to Þórr, rather than Óðinn. Here, the giant name *Dofri* is used when the apparent speaker is Þrymr. See the Introduction to this work, p. xi. — [2] <af galldri>: It is somewhat unclear where this fits into the sense of the rest of the stanza. Have the gods been deceived by magic, does Þrymr speak by magic or has he hidden the hammer with magic? We opt for the last sense.

Stanza I.25

Nema þier freyiu færit mier.	'nema þér Freyju færið mér,
at fegra er hueriu uife.	að fegra er hverju vífi.
þa mun hamarin hittaz hier	Þá mun hamarinn hittast hér
ok hialp so þinu life.	og hjálp svá þínu lífi.

Translation: 'unless you bring me Freyja, who is fairer than every woman; then the hammer will be found here—and so help your life.

Notes: [2] <fegra>: This neuter form is awkward but presumably refers to *víf*. Finnur emends to the expected *fegri*.

Stanza I.26

Þar mun ramlig Rada giord.	'Þar mun rammlig ráðagjörð
Rognes uera j hollu.	Rögnis vera í höllu.
nyu fet nidur j jord.	Níu fet niðr í jörð
nu er hann grafinn med ollu.	nú er hann grafinn með öllu.'

Translation: 'There will be some potent planning in the hall of Rögnir [Óðinn]. Nine feet below the earth it is now completely buried.'

Notes: [1–2]: Presumably, Þrymr is here further elaborating his demand that the gods must make the right choice and give him what he wants. — [3] <nyu>: The scribe normally spells this word with <y> rather than the expected <i>. Jón Helgason (1975, 248) suggests that he wanted to avoid the confusing combination of five minims. — [3] <nyu fet>: Metrically this is deficient and Finnur Jónsson's emendation of <fet> to *feta* still leaves a wildly unmetrical line. The sense is also unexpected since nine feet seems like a rather paltry distance considering Þrymr's boasting here and in III.20. Based on átján rastir from *Þrymskviða*, Jón Helgason (1975, 248) suggests an emendation to *nítján rastir*. The line is certainly corrupt and something like that may well have been the original text — [4] <grafinn>: Corrected in the manuscript from <geymdur> which would also give good sense but is less metrically normal.

Stanza I.27

Æder heim sa jllsku bier.	Æðir heim sá illsku *tér
allur reide bolgenn.	allur reiði-bólginn.
hefur þu nockut hamarenn hier.	'Hefur þú nökkuð hamarinn hér?
huar er hann miolner folgenn.	Hvar er hann Mjöllnir fólginn?'

Translation: The one who expresses evil [Loki] rushes home, all swollen with rage. 'Do you have the hammer here? Where is my Mjöllnir hidden?'

Notes: [1–2]: In the text as preserved, the person described in the first two lines must be Loki while the person speaking in the second half must be Þórr, making for a somewhat rough transition. As Jón Helgason (1975, 244) points out, the association with anger fits Þórr better than Loki and he suggests *heim* may have originally been *fram*. This would, however, leave us with another rough transition between Þrymr speaking in the preceding verse to Þórr being referred to here. — [1] <bier>: The first letter looks like a <b> but is, perhaps, a botched <t>. In any case, <bier> is senseless, so we follow Finnur Jónsson in emending to *tér*. — [4] <hann>: The word suggests familiarity; we use 'my' to give the approximate sense in English.

Stanza I.28

Hamarinn færi ek huergi þier.	'Hamarinn færi eg hvergi þér,
heyre drotter prudar.	—heyri dróttir prúðar—
nema þu freyiu færer mier	"nema þú Freyju færir mér
ok faer mier hana til brudar.	og fáir mér hana til brúðar.'"

Translation: 'By no means do I bring you the hammer—listen, fine people—"unless you bring Freyja to me and give her to me as my bride."'

Notes: [3–4] Jón Helgason (1975, 245) finds the set-up of this stanza, with Loki apparently directly quoting Þrymr within his own speech, so awkward as to suggest a corrupt text. He suggests replacing *hana* in line 4 with *jötni* but this is metrically and semantically difficult.

Stanza I.29

Reidan giordi ʀognes kund	Reiðan gjörði Rögnis kund
rett j þenna tima.	rétt í þenna tíma.
þor geck up áá freyiu fund.	Þórr gekk upp á Freyju fund.
falli þann ueg ʀima.	Falli þann veg ríma.

Translation: Rögnir's son [Þórr] became angry at that very moment. Þórr went up to meet Freyja. May the *ríma* end this way.

Notes: [4] Exactly the same final line is found in *Brönu rímur*, *Vilmundar rímur* and *Tóbías rímur*. Variations of it are found more widely.

II

Stanza II.1

Holdum færi eg herians sneckiu
    hrodrar barda.
fyrst kom upp j freyiu garda.
fiolnes bur med reide harda.

Höldum færi eg Herjans snekkju,
    hróðrar barða.
Fyrst kom upp í Freyju garða
Fjölnis burr með reiði harða.

Translation: To men I bring Herjann's swift vessel, the ship of poetry. First, Fjölnir's son [Þórr] with grim anger comes up to Freyja's dwelling.

Notes: [1] <herians sneckiu>: This kenning for poetry is also found in *Geirarðs rímur* III.1 (*Rs*, II 485) and *Hjálmþérs rímur* V.1 (*Rs*, II 33), in the second instance alliterating with the word *hróðrar* as here. — [1] <hrodrar barda>: Like Finnur Jónsson we take this to be a noun phrase standing in apposition to *Herjans snekkju* and meaning the same thing. But *barði* for 'ship' is quite an archaic usage and unexpected in *rímur*. The poet might have picked the word up from *Nafnaþulur*. Alternatvely, perhaps *barða* is to be understood as the participle of *berja* 'to beat' and then *hróðrar barða* could be taken to mean something like 'smithed out of praise'.

Stanza II.2

Þa nam kallze þesse ord
    uid þellu ueiga.
uilldu nockut jotunnin eiga
ytum giorer hann kosti seiga.

Þá nam *kallsa þessi orð
    við þellu veiga:
'Vildu nökkuð jötuninn eiga?
Ýtum gjörir hann kosti seiga.'

Translation: Then he began to bandy these words with the pine-tree of drinks [woman]: 'Do you want to marry the giant? He offers tough terms.'

Notes: [1] <kallze> There is no way to parse the sentence as preserved. Like Möbius and Finnur Jónsson we emend to an infinitive form. — [1] <þellu ueiga>: Exactly the same kenning is also found in *Hjálmþérs rímur*, *Áns rímur* and *Ektors rímur*.

Stanza II.3

Hann greiner mal en gullaz skordu
    giorer so hlioda.
þigg nu malmm og menit hid goda.
mælte sidan sprundit rioda.

Hann greinir mál en gullhlaðs skorðu
    gjörir svo hljóða.
'Þigg nú málm og menið hið góða,'
mælti síðan sprundið rjóða.

Translation: He explains the problem, but the prop of gold [woman] becomes silent: 'Now accept metal and the good necklace,' said the rosy-cheeked woman.

Notes: [1] <gullaz>: This is a very popular word in kennings for women from *c*.1400. The *rímur* manuscripts usually spell it as <gullaz> or <gullazt>, suggesting that its presumed origin as *gull-hlaðs* is more or less forgotten. The kenning *gullhlaðs skorða* is found more than twenty times in medieval *rímur*. — [2] <malmm>: This presumably refers to gold and/or silver.

Stanza II.4

Fyr skal eg mier fleyia ut	'Fyrr skal eg mér fleyja út
fagran geima.	*í fagran geima
helldur en fara j jota heima.	heldr en fara í *jötna heima.
onguan giorer eg kost æ þeima.	Öngvan gjörir eg kost á þeima.'

Translation: 'Sooner shall I fling myself out into the fair sea, rather than journey to Jötunheimar; by no means is this an option.'

Notes: [1] í: Like Möbius and Finnur Jónsson we add this preposition to fix the sense. — [2] The line is one alliterating position short. — [2] <jota heima>: 'Land of the Jutes'. Like Möbius and Finnur Jónsson we emend to *jötna*. — [3] <giorer>: The use of *r*-final verb forms in the first person is fairly common in Middle Icelandic.

Stanza II.5

Þor nam ganga þrutenn áá burtt	Þórr nam ganga þrútinn á burt
fra þorna gefnne.	frá þorna Gefni.
attle tru eg at einum hefne	Atli trúi eg að einum hefni.
angur stendur honum fyrer suefne	Angur stendur honum fyrir svefni.

Translation: Þórr walked, swollen [with emotion], away from the Gefn of brooches [woman]. I believe Atli [Þórr] will punish someone on account of this. He cannot sleep for grief.

Notes: [1] <þorna gefnne>: This kenning also occurs in *Vilmundar rímur*. Both constituents of it are common in woman kennings, Gefn being the name of a goddess and *þorn* 'thorn, pin' referring to jewellery. — [3] *Atli* is given as a name of Þórr in *Þórs heiti*, another of the *Nafnaþulur* (Gurevich, ed., 2017c, 758) and is used to refer to him in several *rímur*. We have tried to render the line without emending it but the sense is somewhat unclear. Möbius and

Finnur Jónsson emend <attle> to *Atla* and take the line to mean that
Þórr is suffering (1926–28, 162). But the same phrasing occurs in
Mábilar rímur VI.49 with nominative as in the preserved text here:
'bera kann til ad hun einum hefni' (Valgerður Kr. Brynjólfsdóttir
2004, 159).

Stanza II.6

Ma nu ecki milldingssonuren　　　Má nú ekki mildingssonrinn
　　miollne spenna.　　　　　　　　Mjöllni spenna
elldar þottu ur augum brena.　　　eldar þóttu úr augum *brenna
ygldizt rymur uid leiken þenna.　　ygldist Rymur við leikinn þenna.

Translation: Now the king's son [Þórr] cannot clasp Mjöllnir. Fires
seemed to blaze from his eyes. Rymr [Þórr] frowned at this game.

Notes: [2] Þórr's terrible gaze is referred to twice in *Gylfaginning* and
especially in *Húsdrápa* where his eyes are said to shoot beams (Lassen
2003, 108). Kings are often said to have especially sharp eyes in Old
Norse literature (Lassen 2003, 17–18) and this may explain the choice to
refer to Þórr as *mildingssonr* 'king's son' here. — [2] <brena>: A sloppy
spelling of *brenna*. — [3] <rymur>: This name of Þórr also occurs in
Nafnaþulur and *Lokrur*.

Stanza II.7

Odin lætur efna þing　　　　　　Óðinn lætur efna þing
　　áá asa uollum.　　　　　　　　á Ása völlum.
reckar drifu ur Rognnis hollum.　　Rekkar drifu úr Rögnis höllum.
Rædan tokz med godunum ollum.　Ræðan tókst með goðunum öllum.

Translation: Óðinn calls an assembly on the fields of the gods.
Men issued forth out of Rögnir's halls. Speech began amongst all
the gods.

Stanza II.8

Heimdæll gaf til hoskligt rad　　　Heimdæll gaf til horskligt ráð
　　en heyRnar prude.　　　　　　inn heyrnar prúði:
þor skal nefna þussa brude.　　　'Þór skal nefna þursa brúði.
þeim skal ueitazt kuenna skrude.　Þeim skal veitast kvenna skrúði.'

Translation: Heimdæll gave out good advice, the magnificent listener:
'The bride of giants shall be called Þórr. To that one will be granted a
woman's raiment.'

Stanza II.9

Ytar byggiu asa þor
    sem eg uil greina.
settu æ bringu breida steina.
blod rautt gull og pellit hreina

Ýtar *bjuggu Ása-Þór
    sem eg vil greina
settu á bringu breiða steina,
blóðrautt gull og pellið hreina.

Translation: Men prepared Ása-Þórr as I will relate: they set on his breast broad stones, blood-red gold and pure silk.

Notes: The stanzas here given in the order of the manuscript as II.9–II.13 appear in the order 13, 9, 12, 10, 11 in Finnur's *Fernir rímnaflokkar* edition and in the order 13, 12, 9, 10, 11 in his *Rímnasafn* edition. Finnur's rearrangements are quite reasonable (see also Jón Helgason 1975, 245) but we have opted to follow the manuscript, as did Möbius. — [1] <byggiu>: The past subjunctive does not seem to fit here so we emend to the indicative form. — [3] <blod rautt gull>: This phrase occurs in various poems, religious and profane. — [3] <breida steina>: The same phrase appears in the same context in *Þrymskviða* and nowhere else that we have found. The stones in question are presumably gemstones of some sort.

Stanza II.10

Heimdæll biozt ok hęnir med
    hoskr j rędum.
loke uar klæddur kuinu klædum.
klokur þotti hann nesta j rædum.

Heimdæll bjóst og Hænir með,
    horskr í ræðum.
Loki var klæddur *kvinnu klæðum.
Klókur þótti hann næsta í ræðum.

Translation: Heimdæll prepared himself and Hænir too, wise in speech. Loki was clad in women's clothes. He seemed very clever in speech.

Notes: [1] <med> Finnur emends to *meður* to get an extra syllable, but this is undermotivated. The metre occasionally has a monosyllable in this position and a light disyllable would not be any more usual. — [1] <rędum>: The first vowel has an ambiguous appearance and could be read as <ǫ>. — [3] <rædum>: The identical rhyme is suspicious. Jón Helgason (1975, 249) suggests one instance should be *frædum*.

Stanza II.11

Oden atti frabærtt far
    er flutte beima.
ʀan þat ein ueg rust og geima
med reida geck þat um loguna heima

Óðinn átti frábært far
    er flutti beima.
Rann það einn veg rúst og geima.
Með reiða gekk það um löguna heima.

Translation: Óðinn had an excellent vessel which carried men. It ran the same way over hill and sea. With rigging it went over the seas of the worlds.

Notes: It is unclear what source, if any, the poet had for this description of Óðinn's ship. — [2] <rust>: A rare word in pre-Reformation Icelandic. We know of no other instance in poetry, and *ONP* lists only two in prose. — [3] <heima>: Like Jón Helgason (1975, 249), we take this to be genitive plural of the noun *heimr*. Taking it as an adverb, 'at home', seems semantically difficult.

Stanza II.12

Ytar biugiu Asa þor	Ýtar bjuggu Ása-Þór
med ofnnis skide.	með Ofnis skíði.
þesse karllen kampa side	Þessi karlinn kampa-síði
kemr j stad fyrer hringa fridi	kemr í stað fyrir hringa Fríði.

Translation: Men prepared Ása-Þórr with the wooden staves of Ofnir [gold]. This man with long whiskers takes the place of the Fríðr of rings [woman].

Notes: [1] <biugiu>: There are some examples of similar spellings in *ONP* but we have normalised to a form without final <ju>. — [1] <ofnnis skide>: It is not clear whether the spelling of the name should be normalised as Ofnir or as Ófnir. The name appears in *Óðins nǫfn* as a name for Óðinn (Gurevich, ed., 2017b, 748), but seems to have been reanalysed by *rímur* poets as a serpent *heiti* (c.f. the entry for *ófnir* in Finnur Jónsson's *Ordbog til rimer* (1926–28, 283). Gold kennings in the format 'the [flat surface] of the serpent' are abundant in medieval *rímur*, referring to the popular belief that dragons slept on piles of gold. A literary example of such a dragon can be seen in the first chapter of *Ragnars saga loðbrókar* (Rafn, ed., 1829, 235). — [1] <Asa>: A rare example of a stanza-internal capital letter. — [2] <karllen>: Or perhaps <karllenn>; there is a small dot above the <n>. — [3] <hringa fridi>: Exactly the same kenning is found in multiple medieval *rímur*.

Stanza II.13

Buning allan ber þier upp	'Búning allan *beri þér upp
áá beiti sara.	á beiti sára.
þan veg skulv vær þussa dara.	Þann veg skulu vær þursa dára.
þor er like kuenna farra	Þórr er líki kvenna fára.'

Translation: 'You shall dress the user of wounds [man] in all the apparel. In this way we shall fool the giants. Þórr is like few women.'

Notes: [1–4] This stanza would more naturally follow II.8 as a continuation of Heimdæll's plan to disguise Þórr, which is how Finnur Jónsson emends the text (*Rímnasafn* I, 283). — [1] <ber>: We see no way to parse the sentence as preserved and follow previous editors in emending to *beri*. — [1] <beiti sara>: This appears to be a garbled kenning. Jón Helgason (1975, 249) suggests emending to *býti* but *býtir sára* 'distributor of wounds' would still be an unusual kenning. — [3] <farra>: The word could conceivably be read as <frara> though this would make little sense. The word is divided between lines and the abbreviation is atypical.

Stanza II.14

Godunum fylgia geyse marger
    geitur og kalfar.
telzt þa ecki troll ok alfar
tofra menn og uolwor sialfar.

Goðunum fylgja geysi-margar
    geitr og kálfar,
telst þá ekki tröll og álfar,
töframenn og völvur sjálfar.

Translation: Very many goats and calves follow the gods, not counting trolls and elves, magicians and witches themselves.

Notes: The colourful description in stanzas II.14–II.15 is without parallel in *Þrymskviða* or the ballads. It is faintly reminiscent of the Wild Hunt motif, with the gods apparently travelling *en masse* to Þrymr's estate, accompanied by a cavalcade of beasts and beings both supernatural and mundane. Sverrir Tómasson points to these stanzas as an example of how *rímur* could lend themselves to dramatic performance by a group of players (2012, 71–72).

Stanza II.15

Fugllar marger fylgia þeim
    af fleina rogum.
uille dyr af ueide slodum.
uarga sueit med ulfwm nogum.

Fuglar margir fylgja þeim
    af fleina rógum,
villidýr af veiðislóðum,
varga sveit með úlfum nógum.

Translation: Many birds follow them from quarrels of darts [battles], wild beasts from the hunting trails, a pack of beasts with plenty of wolves.

Notes: [1] <fleina rogum>: This is a conventional battle kenning and we take it to indicate that the birds in question are carrion eaters. However, we know of no other instance of *róg* or *rógr* in the plural, which renders this somewhat suspect. Finnur Jónsson emends *þeim af fleina rógum* to *þeima fleina rjóðum* 'those reddeners of spears', a clever solution. — [2] Möbius emends *veiðislóðum* to *veiðiskógum* 'hunting forests' in an effort to straighten out the rhyme. But see the next comment. — [3] Finnur Jónsson emends *nógum* to *óðum* in an effort to get regular rhyme. But there are a number of instances where *g* and *ð* rhyme in the medieval *rímur* so it is not necessarily an indicator of textual corruption. — [4] As modern English lacks an appropriate synonym for 'wolf'—the accurate translation of both *vargr* and *úlfr*—*varga sveit* has here been rendered as 'a pack of beasts'.

Stanza II.16

Þegnar koma j þussa gard
    er þundar heiter.
ute stodv jotnna sueiter.
aller vorv furdu teiter.

Þegnar koma í þursa garð
    er Þundar heitir.
Úti stóðu jötna sveitir.
Allir vóru furðu-teitir.

Translation: The men come to the giants' estate, which is called Þundar. A band of giants stood outside. They were all very cheerful.

Notes: [1] <þundar>: This name is not found elsewhere and might be corrupt.

Stanza II.17

Þvi kom ecki æsa þor
    med ydur til veizlu.
honum mun verda giof til greizlu.
giortt uar slikt at vore beizlu.

'Því kom ekki Ása-Þórr
    með yður til veizlu?
Honum mun verða gjöf til greiðslu,
Gjört var slíkt at várri beiðslu.'

Translation: 'Why has Ása-Þórr not come with you to the feast? He is owed a gift in payment. This was done at our behest.'

Notes: Like Jón Helgason (1975, 245), we take the speaker here to be Þrymr, but Finnur (*Rs*, I 288) takes it to be his men. — [2] <gioftil greizlu>: This phrase also occurs in *Háttatal* 88, also rhyming with *veizlu*.

Stanza II.18

Segguren taladi sæmdar giarn
    vid sina recka.
hamaren velldur hann fær ecka.
heima tru ec hann uilie drecka.

Seggrinn talaði sæmdargjarn
    við sína rekka:
'Hamarinn veldur hann fær ekka.
Heima trúi eg hann vilji drekka!'

Translation: The man, eager for honour, spoke to his men: 'He is sobbing because of the hammer. I expect he wants to stay at home drinking!'

Notes: [1] Jón Helgason (1975, 245) takes the speaker in lines 2–3 to be Loki, but as he himself points out, the first line fits very poorly with this assumption. The text as preserved must be taken to mean that Þrymr turns to his men to answer his own question with a jibe at Þórr's expense.

Stanza II.19

Þegnum heilsar þussa gramur.	Þegnum heilsar þursa gramr,
þrymur j kife.	Þrymr í kífi,
grimmre þotte gaman at life.	*Grímni þótti gaman að lífi,
glotte þegar ok hyggur at vife.	glotti þegar og hyggr að vífi.

Translation: Þrymr, the quarrelsome lord of the giants, greets the men. Life seemed fun to Grímnir [Þrymr]. Already grinning, he turns his attention to the woman.

Notes: Jón Helgason (1975, 245) suggests that the text would be more coherent if stanza II.19 were placed before stanzas II.17–II.18. However, this would spoil the natural transition between stanzas 19 and 20. — [2] <grimmre>: Spelled <grimm^e>. Möbius takes this to be *Grímni* and Finnur follows suit, as do we. But this must count as an emendation; we are not aware of a precedent in the manuscript for superscript <e> standing for <ne> rather than <re>. Indeed, *grimmri* is a perfectly normal word and it even makes for a grammatical sentence here, albeit one that is senseless in the context.

Stanza II.20

Flagda uinuren fifla uill.	Flagða vinrinn fífla vill
til fliods j vagnni.	til fljóðs í vagni.
eigi skylde hann ygllazt magnne.	Eigi skyldi hann yglast magni.
æsum kom nv brogd at gagne	Æsum kom nú brögð að gagni.

Translation: The friend of giantesses [Þrymr] wants to seduce the woman in the wagon. He should not frown greatly. Tricks now come to benefit the Æsir.

Notes: [2] <magnne>: A puzzling word here. In his dictionary (1926–28, 255), Finnur Jónsson takes this to be the noun *magn* 'strength' used in an instrumental sense to mean 'to a high degree'. In his *Rímnasafn* edition (*Rs* I:288) he suggests it might be the proper name Magni, normally a son of Þórr but here referring to Þórr himself. Both solutions seem strained, but we have been unable to come up with anything better and have used the first of Finnur's ideas. — [3] <æsum>: The noun is originally a u-stem, but the sources show much variety in its declension, see *ONP*. — [3] <kom>: A plural *koma* or *komu* would have been more likely. — [3] <nv>: The first letter of this word was read as <n> both by Möbius and Finnur Jónsson and we have no better suggestion. But as an <n> it is highly abnormal, with a long ascender. Finnur suggests it was corrected from a <b> but this is not obvious to us.

Stanza II.21

Kappen uilldi kyssa fliod
    en kynia skiote.
rette hendur en ramme sote.
reygdizt næsta brudr j mote.

Kappinn vildi kyssa fljóð
    inn kynja-skjóti.
Rétti hendr inn rammi sóti.
Reygðist næsta brúðr í móti.

Translation: The strangely quick champion wanted to kiss the lady. The strong giant reached out with his hands. The bride bridled very much at this.

Notes: [2] <sote>: We follow Finnur Jónsson (1926–28, 342) in taking this to mean 'giant' here. However, the word normally means 'horse' and we cannot find another instance where it refers to a giant. — [3] There is a strange flourish after the r-rotunda at the end of <brudr>. It looks like a rum rotunda but a transcription as <brudrum> would not make any sense. The same word is written in this eccentric way in stanzas III.3 and III.16.

Stanza II.22

Bruse sagdi brogden liot
    ǽ bauga þreyiu.
þvi eru endott augu freyiu
ecki lizt oss bragd ǽ meyiu

Brúsi sagði brögðin ljót
    á bauga *eyju.
'Því eru endótt augu Freyju?
Ekki lízt oss bragð á meyju.'

Translation: Brúsi [Þrymr] said the island of rings [woman] had an ugly appearance. 'Why are Freyja's eyes fearsome? This does not seem to us the countenance of a maiden.'

Notes: [1] <þreyiu>: We see no sensible way to understand the manuscript text and follow Finnur Jónsson in emending to *eyju*, yielding a normal woman kenning, also occurring in *Jarlmanns rímur*, *Sturlaugs rímur* and *Skáld-Helga rímur*. — [2] <endott>: Finnur reads the first vowel as an <o> corrected from an <e>. But it looks like an <e> to us and it did to Jón Helgason too (1975, 249). The corresponding sentence in *Þrymskviða* is 'Hví eru ǫndótt / augu Freyju?' (*Eddukvæði*, I 426). Apart from this, the word occurs only in *Húsdrápa*, where it is also used of Þórr's eyes. The *e* vowel in *Þrymlur* could be taken as evidence that the original form was *ǿndóttr* rather than *ǫndóttr*. None of the relevant manuscripts predates the

Þrymlur: The Bearded Bride

ǫ/ø merger and variation between *e* and *ø* is found in a number of words while variation between *e* and *ǫ* is not. The exact sense of the word is unknown.

Stanza II.23

Þetta undrazt þegna sueit	Þetta undrast þegna sveit
huad þrymur red spialla.	hvað Þrymur réð spjalla.
þa slo þognn ā́ þussa alla	Þá sló þögn á þursa alla.
þar mvn bragurenn verda falla.	Þar mun bragrinn verða falla.

Translation: The troop of men wonder about what Þrymr said. Then silence struck all the giants. There the poetry will have to cease.

III

Stanza III.1

ÞAR skal bratt enn þridia mærd.	Þar skal brátt in þriðja mærð
þegna sueit af aflle færd.	þegna sveit af afli færð.
loptur greidde lydum suor.	Loftur greiddi lýðum svör,
longum þotte hann slyngur uid for.	löngum þótti hann slyngur við för.

Translation: Soon the third praise[-poem] shall be vigorously delivered to the troop of men. Loftr [Loki] provided answers to the people; long seemed he clever at journeying.

Notes: [1] *Mærð* appears frequently as a synonym for *poetry* in *rímur*, although apart from later references to beautiful women in the introductory *mansöngr* stanzas, few *rímur* actually function as praise-poems.

Stanza III.2

Ecki suaf hann um atian dægur.	'Ekki svaf *hon um átján dægr,'
odins talade þrælenn slægur.	Óðins talaði þrælinn slægr,
so uar hon hingad freyia fus.	'svá var hon hingað, Freyja, fús
fare nu menn og tialldit hus.	fari nú menn og tjaldið hús.'

Translation: 'She did not sleep for eighteen half-days,' Óðinn's sly thrall [Loki] said, 'so eager was Freyja to travel here. Now people may go and decorate the house with cloth.'

Notes: [1] <hann>: We follow our predecessors in emending to *hon*. — [1] <dægr>: A day or a night—so eighteen *dægr* is nine days. — [2] <þrælenn>: A nominative form with a single *l*, cf. stanza I.21.

Stanza III.3

Sidan settizt brudr ã beck.
baugi allt til ueizlu feck.
bar hon af flestum brvdum stærdd.
bysna digur og alluel hærdd.

Síðan settist brúðr á bekk.
Baugi allt til veizlu fekk.
Bar hon af flestum brúðum stærð,
býsna digr og allvel hærð.

Translation: Then the bride sat herself on a bench. Baugi [Þrymr] got everything for the feast. She surpassed most brides in size, very stout and quite hairy.

Stanza III.4

Loptur suaf hia lauka rein.
leizt hon uera sem þernan ein.
trollen fra eg at toku upp bord.
taladi brvdurenn ecki ord.

Loftur svaf hjá lauka rein.
Leizt hon vera sem þernan ein.
Tröllin frá eg að tóku upp borð.
Talaði brúðrin ekki orð.

Translation: Loftr [Loki] slept by the land of leeks [woman]. She had the appearance of a maidservant. I heard that the trolls took up a table. The bride spoke not a word.

Notes: [1] <suaf>: This word is unexpected. Jón Helgason (1975, 249) suggests an emendation to *sat*, which is certainly tempting. — [1] <lauka rein>: Exactly the same kenning occurs in many medieval *rímur*. — [3] There is a mark that looks like a half-deleted *i* or *r* rotunda above the *t* of *toku*.

Stanza III.5

Aller skipuduz jotnnar tolf|
odrv megin vid hallar golf.
hlaupa vpp med heimsku ã beck.
hefur sa ver at fyrer þeim geck.

Allir skipuðust jötnar tólf
öðru megin við hallargólf,
hlaupa upp með heimsku á bekk.
Hefur sá verr að fyrir þeim gekk.

Translation: All twelve giants arranged themselves on one side of the hall floor. They run up foolishly on the bench—too bad for anyone who gets in their way!

Notes: [1] <tolf|>: Instead of the usual dot, a vertical stroke is used here to separate the verses. The scribe may have accidentally left too little space for a dot between <tolf> and <odrv>.

Stanza III.6

Þar var surtur hake og hrymur.
hôfdingen var jotnna þrymur.
sorkuer mode geiter og glamur.
grimner bruse dofri og amur.

Þar var Surtur, Haki og Hrymr
—höfðinginn var jötna Þrymr–
Sörkvir, Móði, Geitir og Glámr,
Grímnir, Brúsi, Dofri og Ámr.

Translation: There was Surtr, Haki and Hrymr—Þrymr was the chieftain of the giants—Sörkvir, Móði, Geitir and Glámr, Grímnir, Brúsi, Dofri and Ámr.

Notes: The *Nafnaþulur* list Surtr, Geitir, Glámr, Grímnir, Dofri and Ámr as giant names. Hrymr appears as an opponent of the gods, presumably a giant, in *Vǫluspá* (*Eddukvæði*, I 303). The name Haki occurs in a giant-like context in *Hyndluljóð* (*Eddukvæði*, I 466). Brúsi occurs as a giant in *Klerka rímur* (*Rs*, II 888) and *Skíða ríma* 172 (*Rs*, I 36). Some of these also occur as names for other entities, such as sea kings and goats. Móði is not usual as a giant name.

Stanza III.7

Eigi uar þeirra flockuren fridr	Eigi var þeirra flokkrinn fríðr.
fala kom þar jnn og gridur.	Fála kom þar inn og Gríðr,
hlock og syrpa gialp og greip.	Hlökk og Syrpa, Gjálp og Greip.
geyseligt var þeirra sueip.	Geysiligt var þeirra sveip.

Translation: Their band was not beautiful. Fála came in there and Gríðr too, Hlökk and Syrpa, Gjálp and Greip. Their tumult was enormous.

Notes: Gjálp and Greip are also mentioned together in *Snorra Edda* (Finnur Jónsson 1931, 107) and in *Hyndluljóð* (*Eddukvæði*, I 467). Fála, Syrpa and Gríðr are giantesses names found in various sources but Hlökk is usually a valkyrie name. — [1] <flockuren>: The definite article is added in the margin. — [4] <sueip>: We cannot find another instance of *sveip* as a neuter noun, but the masculine noun *sveipr* can mean 'sudden movement' or 'tumult'.

Stanza III.8

Kuomu á bordit bryt trog stor.	Kvámu á borðið bryttrog stór.
bruder satu upp hia þor.	Brúðir sátu upp hjá Þór.
jaxlar veitu jotnnvm lid.	Jaxlar veittu jötnum lið.
eingen hafdi hnifen vid.	Enginn hafði hnífinn við.

Translation: Large butcher's troughs came to the table. The women sat up by Þórr. The giants were assisted by their molars. No one used a knife.

Stanza III.9

Borduzt þeir med bysnnum so.	Börðust þeir með býsnum svá
blodit dreif vm alla þa.	blóðið dreif um alla þá.
knutum uar þar kastad opt.	Knútum var þar kastað oft.
Komv stundum hnefar á lopt.	Komu stundum hnefar á loft.

Translation: They fought so outrageously that the blood spattered all over them. Knucklebones were often thrown there. Sometimes fists were raised.

Notes: This stanza would be improved by switching the first half and the second half around.

Stanza III.10

Wgxa fra eg at æte brudur.
ecki uar þeirra leikurenn prudur.
lagdi hon at sier laxa .tolf.
og let þo alldre bein golf.

Uxa frá eg að æti brúðr.
Ekki var þeirra leikrinn prúðr.
Lagði hon að sér laxa tólf
og lét þó aldri bein á gólf.

Translation: I heard that the bride ate an ox. Their game was not dignified. She consumed twelve salmon and yet never let a bone fall to the floor.

Notes: [1] <æte>: The <t> is smudged. — [2] <ecki>: The <i> at the end is faded and looks like <:>. — [3] <lagdi hon at>: The exact meaning is unclear; we have not found another instance of this turn of phrase. — [4] <þo>: Asded above the line.

Stanza III.11

Undra taca nv jotna sueit.
at og dryck at brudar leit.
fliod er ordit furdu grett.
flagdit talade þannen huertt.

Undra taka nú jötna sveit
át og drykk að brúðar leit.
'Fljóð er orðið furðu *gert,'
flagðið talaði þannin hvert.

Translation: Now the troop of giants begins to wonder. They looked at the bride's eating and drinking. 'The woman has become very greedy,' said each of the ogresses.

Notes: [1] <taka>: A plural verb with a singular subject (*sveit*) sometimes occurs in poetry when the noun has a group sense and the verb does not immediately follow it. — [3] <grett>: We follow the previous editors in emending to *gert*, improving both the sense and the rhyme.

Stanza III.12

Loptur heyrde liotan kur.
leingi suarade nala bur.
huad kan verda hueriu likt.
hafe þier skamm er talit vm slikt.

Loftur heyrði ljótan kurr.
Lengi svaraði nála burr:
'Hvað kann verða hverju líkt.
Hafi þér skamm er talið um slíkt!

Translation: Loftr [Loki] heard the ugly grumbling. The son of needles replied at length: 'One thing can resemble another. Shame on you who speak of such things!

Notes: [1] The order of <liotan kur> and <heyrde> is reversed in the MS and corrected by the scribe. — [2]: <nala bur>: The previous editors, not unreasonably, emend to *Nálar burr* but perhaps Loki could be thought of as a son of many needles. For the association of Loki with needles see Heide 2011. — [3] This line sounds like an idiom, and a similar phrase occurs in *Grettis rímur* III.14: 'mart kann odrv ligt at verda' (*Rs*, I 56). Here Loki may be implying that the giantesses are greedy eaters themselves and not in a position to talk. — [4] <hafe>: Written <h^e>.

Stanza III.13

Fastad hefur hon fiortan nætur.	'Fastað hefr hon fjórtán nætr,
freyia sialf og haluren mætur.	Freyja sjálf og halrinn mætr.
drosen huorke drack ne æt.	Drósin hvárki drakk né át.
driumiog er hon nv orden kat.	Drjúgmjög er hon nú orðin kát.'

Translation: 'She has fasted fourteen nights, Freyja herself and the noble man. The girl neither drank nor ate. She has now become very merry.'

Notes: [2] <haluren mætur>: Finnur Jónsson (*Rs*, I 289) and Jón Helgason (1975, 249) take this to refer to Loki. If so, the text is presumably corrupt. But perhaps the designation is meant to apply to Þrymr with the poet envisioning a custom of both the bride and the groom fasting before a wedding.

Stanza III.14

Faunzt vær eigi j forze nv.	'Fáumst vér eigi í forzi nú.
furdu jll er skemtan su.	Furðu ill er skemmtan sú.'
brvse talade bragda forn.	Brúsi talaði bragða forn:
bere þier jnn hit mickla horn.	'Beri þér inn hið mikla horn!'

Translation: 'Let us not exert ourselves in anger now; that sort of entertainment is very bad.' Brúsi [Þrymr] spoke, sly and ancient: 'Carry in the great horn!'

Notes: [1–2] It is not clear whether the speaker here is Loki or Þrymr, although as it is more common for speakers to change at the end of a stanza, rather than halfway through, Þrymr seems the more likely choice.

Stanza III.15

Kom sa inn er krasar mat.	Kom sá inn er krásar mat
og kenner þegar huar brudurenn sat.	og kennir þegar hvar brúðrin sat.

| hafdi æ ser hofuden þriv. | Hafði á sér höfuðin þrjú. |
| hrædder mundu flester nu. | Hræddir mundu flestir nú. |

Translation: The one who prepares delicious food came in and immediately recognised where the bride sat. He had three heads on him. Most would now be afraid.

Notes: [1] <krasar>: This rare verb is also found in *Haralds rímur Hringsbana* V.35 (Ólafur Halldórsson 1973, 51).

Stanza III.16

Furdu var þat hornit hatt.	Furðu var það hornið hátt
er hafli tok vit einkar bratt.	er Hafli tók við einkar brátt.
byrllara þeim er bavgi gaf.	Byrlara þeim er Baugi gaf
brudren drack j einv af.	brúðrin drakk í einu af.

Translation: That horn was very tall, which Hafli seized with great speed. The bride downed in one the drink-bringer which Baugi gave.

Notes: [2] <hafli>: This is a giant name in the *Nafnaþulur* as well as in *Lokrur* so presumably it refers here to the cook, who is receiving the horn and passing it on to the bride. — [3–4] We follow Finnur Jónsson in construing these lines as: 'brúðrin drakk í einu af þeim byrlara er baugi gaf', taking *byrlari* to refer to the horn. This is problematic, since *byrlari* normally means 'cup-bearer'.

Stanza III.17

Krassar þegar at komv til	Krásar þegar að komu til
kena red þær menia bil.	kenna réð þær menja Bil.
segger toku at segia j senn.	Seggir tóku að segja í senn:
salld af miodinum drack hon enn.	'Sáld af mjöðinum drakk hon enn!'

Translation: When delicacies appeared, the Bil of necklaces [woman] tasted them. The men began to say all at once: 'Yet again she drank a measure of mead!'

Notes: [2] <menia bil>: Exactly the same kenning occurs dozens of times in the medieval *rímur*. Bil appears in *Gylfaginning* as one of two children who are said to follow the moon across the skies and she is later counted among the Ásynjur (Faulkes, ed., 2005, 14; 30). 'The [goddess name] of [decorative items]' is a very common kenning for women across the *rímur* corpus. — [2] <miodinum>: The older form is *miðinum* but the u-stem inflection has weakened by the time of our manuscript.

Stanza III.18

Kallar þrymur ã kappa sin.	Kallar Þrymr á kappa sín:
kome þier fram j heller min.	'Komi þér fram í hellir mín!
mæle þier at moder wor.	Mæli þér að móðir vár
meyiv færi gefnar tar.	meyju færi Gefnar tár.

Translation: Þrymr called to his champions: 'Come forth into my cave! Tell our mother to bring the maiden the tear of Gefn [gold].'

Notes: [1–2] <sin>, <min>: The possessive pronouns are sometimes left uninflected in *rímur* and ballads when this aids the rhyme. — [2] <hellir>: A young accusative form, probably reflecting the language of the scribe rather than that of the poet. — [4] <gefnar tar>: A common kenning for gold, occurring in several other *rímur*. In *Skáldskaparmál*, we are told that gold may be referred to as *grátr Freyju* 'Freyja's weeping', and *Gylfaginning* says that Freyja wept tears of red gold when separated from her husband Óðr (Faulkes, ed., 2005, 29; 2007, 40; 43). Substituting one goddess name for another is standard practice in *rímur* kennings.

Stanza III.19

Kelling þesse kemur j holl.	Kerling þessi kemr í höll.
knytt er hon og bomlud oll.	Knýtt er hún og bömluð öll.
hafdi hon uetur um hundrat þren.	Hafði hon vetr um hundrað þrenn.
hverge uar hun þo bognud enn.	Hvergi var hon þó bognuð enn.

Translation: This old woman comes into the hall. She is knotted and twisted all over. She had lived one winter in addition to three hundred, yet she was not at all bowed.

Notes: [1] *kemur* was originally omitted in the line but the scribe has added the word in the margin and an insertion sign between <þesse> and <j>. — [2] <hon>: Since the metre requires a long vowel here, we have normalised the word to *hún*. — [2] <bomlud>: Apart from this instance, this word seems to occur only in *Bósa saga* and *Bósa rímur*, in these texts describing a shield-maiden who has recovered from serious wounds ('ok var hún síðan hnýtt ok bömluð', Jiriczek 1893, 5; 'bomlud uar hun en beininn liot / bradliga giordi at hnyta', Ólafur Halldórsson 1974, 40).

Stanza III.20

Syrpa eg uil senda þig	'Syrpa, eg vil senda þig,
sækia skaltu hamar fyrer mig.	sækja skaltu hamar fyrir mig
nidur j jardar nedsta part.	niðr í jarðar neðsta part.'
nu mun uerda leikit martt.	Nú mun verða leikið mart.

Translation: 'Syrpa, I want to send you down into the lowest part of the earth. You must fetch the hammer for me.' Now there will be much play.

Notes: The speaker is Þrymr. The fourth line might also be part of his speech.

Stanza III.21

Hvergi gatu hamarin færtt.	Hvergi gátu hamarinn fært
hundrat manz þo til se hrætt.	hundrað manns þó til sé *hrært.
keila sette upp kryppu bein.	Keila setti upp kryppu bein.
kerlling gat þo borit hann ein.	Kerling gat þó borið hann ein.

Translation: By no means could the hammer be moved, though a hundred men attempt to shift it. Keila raised the bone of her hump. Yet the old woman could carry it [the hammer] on her own.

Notes: [2] <hrætt>: We follow previous editors in emending to *hrært*, fixing the sense and the rhyme. — [3] *Keila* is given as the name of a female giant in *Skáldskaparmál*, citing an otherwise unknown verse by Þorbjörn dísarskáld in which Þórr's giant-slaying prowess is detailed (Faulkes, ed., 2007, 17). Keila's bony hump is more mysterious, but is perhaps due to a general trend in both prose romances and *rímur* to describe giants and dwarfs as being disfigured in some way. In modern Icelandic, *keila* means 'cone' and the name may be chosen deliberately here.

Stanza III.22

Hamarin kom j hollina stor.	Hamarinn kom í höllina stórr.
huortt mun nockut glediazt þor.	Hvárt mun nökkuð gleðjast Þórr!
mæren þrifur miollner uidur.	Mærin þrífur Mjöllnir viðr.
marger drapv skeggi nidur.	Margir drápu skeggi niðr.

Translation: The big hammer came into the hall. Is Þórr ever happy about this! The maiden catches hold of Mjöllnir. Many bit the dust.

Notes: [4] <drapv skeggi nidur>: The expression, literally 'they struck down with their beards', suggests sadness, defeat or death. We translate it with an English idiom with similar connotations.

Stanza III.23

Sundur j midiv borden brytur.	Sundr í miðju borðin brýtr.
bravd og uin um golfit hrytur.	Brauð og vín um gólfið hrýtr.
jotnnvm uesnar helldur j hug.	Jötnum versnar heldr í hug.
hiartad þeirra er komit ã flug.	Hjartað þeirra er komið á flug.

Translation: He breaks the tables apart down the middle. Bread and wine tumble to the floor. It gets rather worse for the giants' mood; their hearts are taking flight.

Stanza III.24

Bravt hann j sundur j beslu hrygg.	Braut hann í sundr í Beslu hrygg.
brudurin fell þar eigi dygg.	Brúðrin fell þar eigi dygg.
sidan lemur hann trollen tolf.	Síðan lemr hann tröllin tólf.
tennur hriota um hallar golf.	Tennur hrjóta um hallar gólf.

Translation: He broke apart Besla's spine. The unworthy woman fell there. Then he strikes twelve trolls; teeth were scattered across the hall floor.

Notes: [1] According to *Gylfaginning*, Besla (sometimes spelt *Bestla*) is the daughter of the giant Bölþorn. She married Börr and was the mother of Óðinn, Vili and Vé (Faulkes, ed., 2005, 11). The Besla here is probably intended as a generic giantess rather than Óðinn's mother, although the poet (as well as any audience members well-versed in mythological genealogies) may well have been amused by the thought of this awkward family reunion, Þórr being the original Besla's grandson.

Stanza III.25

Æseligur uar ása þor	Æsiligur var Ása-Þórr.
upp mvn reiddur hamarenn stor.	Upp mun reiddur hamarinn stórr.
sette hann nidur á saudungs kinn.	Setti hann niðr á Sauðungs kinn.
sock hann þegar j hausen jnn.	Sökk hann þegar í hausinn inn.

Translation: Ása-Þórr was furious. The big hammer is raised up. It came down on Sauðungr's cheek. It sank immediately into his skull.

Notes: [1] <þor> The word is inserted from the margin. [3] In the *rímur* corpus, the name *Sauðungr* appears both as a giant name, especially in gold kennings of the 'speech of the giants' kind, and as a name for Óðinn (Finnur Jónsson 1926–28, 310). Here the name presumably refers to a giant, who may or may not be Þrymr himself (c.f. the note on *Besla* in III.24 above).

Stanza III.26

Pustrad hefur hann pillta rymur.	Pústrað hefr hann pilta, Rymr.
prettum uar leikenn skalkuren þrymur.	Prettum var leikinn skálkrinn Þrymr.
hann feck hogg þat hausen tok.	Hann fekk högg það hausinn tók.
hofudit fast med aflle skok.	Höfuðið fast með afli skók.

Translation: Rymr [Þórr] has boxed boys' ears. The rogue Þrymr was deceived with tricks. He received a blow that caught the skull. The head shook soundly with the force of the blow.

Notes: [1] *Rymr* is listed as a name of Þórr in the *Þórs heiti* part of the *Nafnaþulur* (Gurevich, ed., 2017c, 758). — [1] <prettum>: Written <p̄ttū>.

Stanza III.27

Þrymlur heite þetta spil.	Þrymlur heiti þetta spil.
þanveg geck vm hamarenn til.	Þannveg gekk um hamarinn til.
eignizt sa sem odar bidur.	Eignist sá sem óðar biðr.
ecki skal þeim kasta nidur.	Ekki skal þeim kasta niðr.

Translation: This game is to be called 'Þrymlur'; that's how it went down with the hammer. The one who requests poetry for himself shall have it. This shall not be cast aside.

Notes: [1] <Þrymlur>: It is uncommon for *rímur* cycles to be named within the texts themselves. A close analogy is *Lokrur* which is also named as such in the last stanza (*Rs*, I 309) with a similar derivation from a giant's name. Other *rímur* cycles named in their last or penultimate stanzas include *Klerka rímur* (*Rs*, II 893), *Filippó rímur* (*RR*, 61) and *Virgiless rímur* (*Rs,* II 858) which are named *Klerkaspil*, *Krítar þáttr* and *Glettudiktar* respectively. In these cases, modern scholarship has tended not to use the poets' preferred names. — [1] <þetta>: The word is supplied in the margin.

GLOSSARY

All words in the normalised text are glossed except personal pronouns (unless the usage is particularly unusual). Prepositional phrases are given under their associated noun or verb. For common words like prepositions, only unusual usage examples are given. References to the text are given in the form *ríma*.stanza.line.

á *prep.* to, onto

að *conj.* that

að *prep.* to, towards

af *prep.* from, of; ahead of III.3.3, III.16.4; by I.2.2, I.24.2

afl *n.* strength III.1.2; III.26.4

aftr *adv.* back I.16.3

ágætr *adj.* great I.6.2

aldri *adv.* never I.24.4, III.10.4

álfr *m.* elf II.14.2

alin *f.* (*see also* **öln**) ell I.5.3

allr *pron.* all, everything I.8.3, I.23.1, I.27.2, II.7.3, II.23.1, II.23.2, III.3.2, III.5.1, III.19.2; everyone I.14.4, II.16.3, III.9.2; *með öllu* entirely I.26.4

allvel *adj.* pretty well III.3.4

angr *n.* grief II.5.3

annar *pron.* other I.1.4, III.5.2

áss *m.* one of the Æsir, a god I.20.1, II.7.1, II.20.3

át *n.* the act of eating III.11.2

átján *num.* eighteen III.2.1

átta *num.* eight I.5.3

auga *n.* eye II.6.2, II.22.2

bamlaðr *adj.* twisted III.19.2

barði *m.* a kind of ship II.1.1

barn *n.* child I.3.4

baugr *m.* ring I.21.2, II.22.1

beiðsla *f.* behest II.17.3

beimar *m.pl.* (poet.) men I.18.2, II.11.1

bein *n.* bone III.10.4, III.21.3

beitir *m.* user II.13.1

bekkr *m.* bench III.3.1, III.5.3

bera *v.* to carry I.6.4, II.13.1, III.3.3,III.14.4, III.21.4

berjast *v.* to fight III.9.1

biðja *v.* to request III.27.3

birtast *v.* to appear I.13.1

blíðr *adj.* cheerful, happy I.10.2

blóð *n.* blood III.9.2

blóðrauðr *adj.* blood-red II.9.3

bognaðr *adj.* stooped, bowed over III.19.4

bólginn *adj.* swollen I.27.2

borð *n.* table III.4.3, III.8.1, III.23.1

bráð *f.* meat, prey I.1.2

bráðr *adj.* quick I.17.1, III.1.1, III.16.2

bragð *n.* trickery, deceit I.13.1, I.13.4, I.19.2, II.20.3, II.22.1, II.22.3; appearance III.14.3

bragnar *m. pl.* (*poet.*) men I.13.2

brauð *n.* bread III.23.2

breiðr *adj.* broad II.9.2

brenna *v.* to burn II.6.2

bringa *f.* breast, chest II.9.2

brjóta *v.* to break III.23.1, III.24.1

brúðr *f.* bride I.28.2, II.8.2, II.21.3, III.3.1, III.3.3, III.4.4, III.8.2, III.10.1, III.11.2, III.15.2, III.16.4; (*poet.*) woman III.24.2

bryttrog *n.* chopping trough III.8.1

búa *v.* to prepare II.9.1, II.10.1, II.12.1

búningr *m.* apparel II.13.1

burr *m.* son I.5.2, I.7.2, II.1.3, III.12.3

burt *adv.* away; **á burt** away II.5.1

byrlari *m.* drink-bearer (*usually a person, but here most plausibly referring to the vessel itself*) III.16.3

býsn *f.* and *n.* wonder, *here used as a general intensifier* III.9.1

býsnadigr *adj.* marvellously stout III.3.4

bæði *pron.* both I.7.3

dára *v.* to fool II.13.2

digr *adj.* stout I.12.4

dóttir *f.* daughter I.3.3

drekka *v.* to drink II.18.3, III.13.3, III.16.4, III.17.4

drepa *v.* to strike; **drápu skeggi niður** they turned their beards down, were dismayed, bit the dust III.22.4

drífa *v.* to issue forth II.7.2, III.9.2

drjúgmjög *adv.* very much I.24.1, III.13.4

drjúgr *adj.* much I.19.2

drós *f.* (*poet.*) girl III.13.3

drótt *f.* people I.28.2

drykkr *m.* drink, the act of drinking III.11.2

dvergr *m.* dwarf I.6.1

dyggr *adj.* worthy III.24.2

dylja *v.* to deceive, keep in ignorance I.24.1

dægr *n.* half a day, twelve hours III.2.1

dæll *adj.* easy to get along with I.21.1

ef *conj.* if I.17.3

efla *v.* (*poet.*) to do I.3.2; to strengthen I.4.4

efna *v.* to establish II.7.1

efni *n.* substance; **í efni** in the offing I.13.4

eftir *adv.* again I.17.4

eiga *v.* to own I.10.3, II.11.1; to marry II.2.2

eigi *adv.* (*see also* **ekki**) not I.3.1, II.20.2, III.7.1, III.14.1, III.24.2

eignast *v.* to come to own III.27.3

einkar *adv.* very III.16.2

einn *num. and pron.* one III.16.4; the same I.20.2, II.11.2, III.4.2; alone III.21.4

ekki *adv.* (*see also* **eigi**) not II.18.2

ekki *m.* lamentation II.18.2

eldr *m.* fire II.6.2

en *conj.* and, but I.1.4

endóttr *adj.* fearsome(?) II.22.2

engi *pron.* (*see also* **öngvan**) no one I.14.3, III.8.4

enn *adv.* yet, still III.17.4, III.19.4

er *pron.* who, which I.1.2, I.6.1, II.16.1, III.12.4, III.16.2, III.16.3

éta *v.* to eat III.10.1, III.13.3

ey *f.* island II.22.1

fá *v.* to get, obtain I.1.2, I.14.1, I.28.4, II.18.2, III.3.2, III.14.1, III.26.3

fagr *adj.* beautiful I.15.1, II.4.1; **fegri** more beautiful I.25.2

falla *v.* to end I.29.4; to fall II.23.3, III.24.2

far *n.* ship II.11.1

fár *adj.* few II.13.3; **fæstur** fewest I.19.1

fara *v.* to travel I.12.3, I.14.2, I.18.3, I.23.1, II.4.2, III.2.4

fasta *v.* to fast III.13.1

fastr *adj.* sound, secure III.26.4

fela *v.* to conceal I.24.3

fet *n. unit of measurement*: foot, pace I.26.3

fífla *v.* to seduce II.20.1

finna *v.* to find I.23.4

finnast *v.* to encounter I.9.2, I.24.4

fjaðrhamr *m.* feather-shape, some sort of bird-costume granting the wearer the power of flight I.16.1, I.17.1, I.19.3

Glossary and Index of Names 37

fjórtán *num.* fourteen III.13.1

flagð *n.* giantess II.20.1, III.11.4

fleinn *m.* missile, arrow II.15.1

fleiri *adj. comp.* more I.9.2; **flestr** most I.4.2, III.3.3, III.15.4

fleyja *v.* to fling II.4.1

fljóð *n.* (*poet.*) woman I.17.2, II.20.1, II.21.1, III.11.3

fljúga *v.* to fly I.16.2, I.18.4, I.19.4, I.20.1

flokkr *m.* group III.7.1

flug *n.* flight III.23.4

flytja *v.* to transport II.11.1

fold *f.* earth I.11.2

fólginn *adj.* concealed I.27.4

forn *adj.* old, ancient III.14.3

forz *n.* fury III.14.1

frá *prep.* from I.13.3, I.23.3, II.5.1

frábærr *adj.* excellent II.11.1

fram *adv.* forwards I.21.1, III.18.2

fregna *v.* to hear of I.6.3, I.8.1, III.4.3, III.10.1

frétt *f.* news I.22.4, I.23.1

fríðr *adj.* handsome, beautiful III.7.1

frægð *f.* fame I.4.4

frægr *adj.* famous I.1.1, I.2.2

frændi *m.* kinsman I.2.1

fugl *m.* bird I.18.3, II.15.1

fundr *m.* meeting I.29.3

furðu *adv.* very, *used as a general intensifier* I.17.1, I.21.1, II.16.3, III.11.3, III.14.2, III.16.1

fúss *adj.* eager III.2.3

fylgja *v.* to accompany II.14.1, II.15.1

fyrir *prep.* in front of III.5.4; in place of II.5.3, III.20.2

fyrr *adv.* before II.4.1; **fyrst** first I.15.2, I.23.2, II.1.2

færa *v.* to bring, convey I.25.1, I.28.1, I.28.3, II.1.1, III.1.2, III.18.4, III.21.1

för *f.* journey, journeying III.1.4

gagn *n.* benefit II.20.3

galdr *m.* magic II.20.3

gaman *n.* fun II.19.2

ganga *v.* to walk, go I.7.1, I.15.2, I.29.3, II.5.1, II.11.3, III.5.4, III.27.2

garðr *m.* enclosure I.15.1, I.20.1, II.1.2, II.16.1

garpr *m.* (*poet.*) man I.11.1, I.19.2

gefa *v.* to give II.8.1, III.16.3

geimi *m.* sea I.20.2, II.4.1, II.11.2

geit *f.* goat II.14.1

gerr *adj.* greedy III.11.3

geta *v.* to be able to III.21.1, III.21.4

geysi *adv.* very, *used as a general intensifier* II.14.1

geysiligr *adj.* enormous III.7.4

gjöf *f.* gift II.17.2

gjöra *v.* to do, make I.10.4, I.29.1, II.2.3, II.3.1, II.4.3, II.17.3

gjörð *f.* girdle I.9.1

gleðjast *v.* to become happy III.22.2

glófi *m.* glove I.10.3, I.11.1

glotta *v.* to smile unpleasantly II.19.3

goð *n.* god II.7.3, II.14.1

góðr *adj.* good II.3.2

gólf *n.* floor III.10.4, III.23.2

grafinn *adj.* buried I.26.4

gramr *m.* lord I.12.4, II.19.1

granda *v.* to hurt, damage, destroy I.19.1

gráta *v.* to cry I.16.4

greiða *v.* to provide III.1.3

greiðsla *f.* bargain, payment II.17.2

greina *v.* to explain, tell I.9.1, II.3.1, II.9.1

greypa *v.* to cover I.11.2

gripr *m.* treasure, valuable possession I.9.2

gull *n.* gold II.9.3

gullhlað *n.* gold lace II.3.1

gumnar *m.pl.* (*poet.*) men I.19.1

hafa *v.* to have I.2.3, I.19.3, I.22.4, I.24.3, I.27.3, III.5.4, III.8.4, III.12.4, III.13.1, III.15.3, III.19.3, III.26.1

hallargólf *n.* hall floor III.5.2, III.24.4

halr *m.* (*poet.*) man I.12.1, III.13.2

hamar *m.* hammer I.6.3, I.13.3, I.14.1, I.16.3, I.17.3, I.23.3, I.24.3, I.25.3, I.27.3, I.28.1, II.18.2, III.20.2, III.22.1, III.25.2, III.27.2

hár *n.* hair I.8.4

hár *adj.* high I.19.4, tall III.16.1; **hæri** louder I.8.3

hærðr *adj.* hairy III.3.4

harðr *adj.* hard I.5.1, I.11.3, II.1.3

harki *m.* tumult, noise, damage, harshness, rubbish; **harka-börn** rascals, scoundrels I.3.4

haugr *m.* mound I.21.4

haukr *m.* hawk; **hauka fold** land of hawks > hand I.11.2

hauss *m.* skull, head III.25.4, III.26.3

hefna *v.* to punish II.5.2

heill *adj.* well, hale I.22.3

heilsa *v.* to greet II.18.1

heim *adv.* homewards I.27.1

heima *adv.* at home II.18.3

heimboð *n.* invitation I.12.1

heimska *f.* foolishness; **með heimsku** foolishly III.5.3

heimr *m.* world I.20.4, II.4.2, II.11.3
heift *f.* feud, hatred I.7.1
heita *v.* to be called I.3.3, I.6.3, I.8.1, I.12.3, II.16.1, III.27.1
heldr *adv.* rather II.4.2, III.23.3
hellir *m.* cave III.18.2
henta *v.* to collect, pick up I.16.3
hér *adv.* here I.13.4, I.25.3, I.27.3
heyra *v.* to hear I.8.3, I.28.2, III.12.1
heyrn *f.* hearing II.8.2
hingað *adv.* hither I.22.3, III.2.3
hitta *v.* to meet, hit upon I.14.3, I.17.3
hjá *prep.* beside III.4.1, III.8.2
hjálpa *v.* to help I.25.4
hjalt *n.* hilt; **hjalta kólfr** bolt of the hilt > sword I.5.1
hjarta *n.* heart III.23.4
hlaupa *v.* to leap, run III.5.3
hljóðr *adj.* silent II.3.1
hnefi *m.* fist III.9.4
hnífr *m.* knife III.8.4
horn *n.* III.14.4, III.15.1
horskligr *adj.* wise II.8.1
horskr *adj.* wise II.10.1
hrafn *m.* raven I.1.2
hreinn *adj.* clean, pure II.9.3
hrífa *v.* to take hold of, grip I.11.3
hringr *m.* ring II.12.3
hrjóta *v.* to tumble III.23.3, III.24.4
hryggr *m.* spine III.24.1
hræddr *adj.* afraid III.15.4
hræra *v.* to shift, cause to move III.21.2

hugr *m.* mind, spirit, thought III.23.3
hundrað *n.* hundred III.19.3, III.21.2
hús *n.* house, building III.2.4
hvað *pron.* what III.12.3
hvar *adv.* where I.14.2, I.27.4, III.15.2
hvárgi *pron.* neither III.13.3
hvárr *pron.* which; **hvárt** whether III.22.2
hverr *pron.* who I.17.4; **hverju** every I.25.2, III.12.3; **hvert** each III.11.4
hverfa *v.* to disappear I.13.3, I.23.3
hvergi *adv.* nowhere I.14.1, I.23.4, I.28.1, III.19.4, III.21.1
hyggja *v.* to think about III.19.3
höfðingi *m.* chieftain III.6.2
höfuð *n.* head I.5.4, III.15.3, III.26.4
högg *n.* blow III.26.3
höldar *m.pl.* (*poet.*) men I.12.2, II.1.1
höll *f.* hall I.7.1, I.26.2, II.7.2, III.19.1, III.22.1, III.24.4
hönd *f.* hand I.11.4, II.21.2

í *prep.* in, to I.20.3, I.20.4
illska *f.* wickedness I.27.1
illr *adj.* bad, wicked I.20.3, III.14.2
inn *prep.* in III.14.4, III.15.1, III.25.4
inn *art.* the I.1.1 *etc.*
inna *v.* to expound I.23.2

jafnan *adv.* always I.18.1
jaxl *m.* molar III.8.3
jungr *adj.* (*see also* **ungr**) young I.7.2
jörð *f.* earth I.26.3, III.20.3
jötunn *m.* giant I.14.3, I.20.4, I.21.4, II.2.2, II.4.2, II.16.2, III.5.1, III.8.3, III.11.1, III.23.3

kálfr *m.* calf II.14.1
kalla *v.* to call out III.18.1
kallsa *v.* to banter, mock II.2.1
kampr *m.* moustache II.12.2
kappi *m.* champion, hero I.6.4, I.8.1, II.21.1, III.18.1
karl *m.* man, fellow I.20.3, I.22.4, II.12.2
kasta *v.* to throw III.9.3, III.27.4
kátr *adj.* cheerful III.13.4
kenna *v.* to recognise III.15.2, III.17.2
kerling *f.* old woman III.19.1, III.21.4
kíf *n.* strife II.19.1
kinn *f.* cheek III.25.3
klókr *adj.* clever II.10.3
klæða *v.* to dress II.10.2
klæði *n.pl.* clothes II.10.2
knúta *f.* knucklebone III.9.3
knýttr *adj.* knotted, twisted III.19.2
kólfr *m.* bolt, tongue; **hjalta kólf** bolt of the hilt > sword I.5.1
koma *v.* to come I.3.1, I.20.4, I.22.3, II.1.2, II.17.1, III.7.2, III.8.1, III.9.4, III.15.1, III.19.1, III.23.4
kona *f.* woman II.8.3, II.13.3
kostr *m.* choice, terms II.2.3, II.4.3
krás *f.* a delicacy III.17.1
krása *v.* to prepare delicacies III.15.1
kryppa *f.* hump, hunch I.20.3, III.21.3
kundr *m.* son, kinsman I.10.3, I.29.1
kunna *v.* to know how to III.12.3
kurr *m.* grumbling III.12.1
kynjaskjótr *adj.* strangely quick II.21.1
kyssa *v.* to kiss II.21.1

láð *n.* (*poet.*) land I.14.3

land *n.* land I.20.2; **landa baugr** ring of lands, *an unclear kenning,* sea? shores? I.21.2

langr *adj.* long, tall I.4.1, III.1.4

láta *v.* to cause something to happen I.6.1, I.16.2, II.7.1, III.10.4; to sound I.8.3

laukr *m.* leek; **lauka rein** land of leeks > woman III.4.1

lax *m.* salmon III.10.3

leggja *v.* to place; **lagði at sér** consumed III.10.3

leiða *v.* to lead I.22.2

leika *v.* to play, trick I.4.2, I.17.2, III.20.4

leikr *m.* game II.6.3, III.10.2, III.26.2

leit *f.* search I.18.1

leita *v.* to search I.17.4

lemja *v.* to strike III.24.3

lengi *adv.* at length III.12.2

lið *n.* assistance, support III.8.3

líf *n.* life I.25.4, II.19.2

líki *m.* equal, likeness II.13.3

líkr *adj.* alike III.12.3

list *f.* art, craft, skill; **með listum** skilfully I.5.2

líta *v.* to look at III.11.2

lítast *v.* to seem II.22.3, III.4.2

ljá *v.* to lend I.16.1

ljótr *adj.* ugly I.22.1, II.22.1, III.12.1

loft *n.* air, sky III.9.4

lýðr *m.* people III.1.3

lymskufullr *adj.* full of cunning I.1.3

lyndi *n.* mind, disposition I.22.1

læsa *v.* to lock, fasten I.19.3

lögr *m.* liquid, sea I.20.2, II.11.3

maðr *m.* man I.7.3, III.2.4, III.21.2

magn *n.* strength (*here used as an intensifier*) II.20.2

mál *n.* problem I.10.2; speech II.3.1

málmr *m.* metal II.3.2

margr *pron.* many, much I.2.3, II.14.1, II.15.1, III.20.4, III.22.4

matr *m.* food III.15.1

með *prep.* with II.7.3, II.10.1, II.11.3, III.26.4; **með** + *dative should be read adverbially* I.4.2, I.5.2, I.26.4, III.5.3

mega *v.* to be able to I.17.3, I.23.4, II.6.1

megin *adv.* to one side III.5.2

meiðast *v.* to come to harm I.7.3

mein *n.* harm I.11.1

meiri *adj.* more I.9.4

men *n.* necklace II.3.2, III.17.2

miðr *adj.* middle III.23.1

mikill *adj.* great III.14.4

mildingr *m.* (*poet.*) king, generous man II.6.1

minn *pron.* my III.18.2

mjór *adj.* thin, slender I.4.1

mjöðr *m.* mead III.17.4

móðir *f.* mother I.2.4, III.18.3

mold *f.* earth I.11.4

mót *n.* meeting; **í móti** against II.21.3

munu *v.* will, must I.3.3, I.24.4, I.25.3, I.26.1, II.17.2, II.23.3, III.15.4, III.20.4, III.22.2, III.25.2

mæði *f.* sorrow, distress I.15.4

mæla *v.* to speak I.2.3, II.3.3, III.18.3

mær *f.* maiden II.22.3, III.18.4, III.22.3

mærð *f.* praise, poetry III.1.1

mætr *adj.* noble III.13.2

ná *v.* to obtain I.14.1

nafn *n.* name I.1.4

nál *f.* needle (*but should perhaps be read as a proper name* **Nál**) III.12.2

nátt *f.* night III.13.1

nauð *f.* need, distress I.8.2

neðstr *adj.* lowest III.20.3

nefna *v.* to name II.8.2

nema *conj.* unless I.25.1, I.28.3

nema *v.* to take; **nema** + *infinitive* to begin to do something I.15.2, II.2.1, II.5.1

niðr *adv.* down III.20.3, III.22.4, III.25.3, II.27.4

níu *num.* nine I.26.3

nóg *adv.* enough II.15.3

nú *adv.* now I.26.4, II.3.2, II.20.3, III.2.4, III.11.1, III.13.4, III.14.1, III.15.4, III.20.4

næsta *adv.* closest, *used as an intensifier* II.21.3

næstr *adj.* closest II.10.3

nökkur *pron.* someone, something I.27.3, II.2.2, III.22.2

óðr *m.* poetry III.27.3

oft *adv.* often III.9.3

og *conj.* and

orð *n.* word I.22.2, II.2.1, III.4.2

pell *n.* expensive fabric, silk II.9.3

piltr *m.* lad III.26.1

prettr *m.* trick, deceit I.3.2, III.26.2

prúðr *adj.* fine, noble I.28.2, II.8.1, III.10.2

pústra *v.* to box someone's ears III.26.1

ráð *n.* advice, counsel II.8.1

ráða *v.* to speak, direct; *ráða* + *infinitive an emphatic* 'did' II.23.1, III.17.2

ráðagjörð *f.* plan-making I.26.1
rammligr *adj.* strong I.26.1
rammr *adj.* strong II.21.2
reiði *f.* anger I.27.2, II.1.3
reiði *m.* rigging II.11.3
rein *f.* strip of land III.4.1
rekkar *m.pl.* (*poet.*) men II.7.2, II.18.1
renna *v.* to run II.11.2
rétt *adv.* precisely, correctly I.29.2
rétta *v.* to reach out II.21.2
reygjast *v.* to bridle, show displeasure II.21.3
ríða *v.* (*here*) to strike I.7.4, III.25.2
ríma *f.* fit of poetry, cycle of *ríma* stanzas I.29.4
rist *f.* instep of the foot I.5.4
rjóða *v.* to redden I.5.1
rjóðr *adj.* red, rosy-cheeked II.3.3
róg *n.* quarrel II.15.1
rúst *f.* hill II.11.2
ræða *f.* speech II.7.3, II.10.1, II.10.3

sá *pron.* that one I.12.3, I.27.1, III.5.4, III.14.2, III.15.1, III.27.3
sáld *n.* measure III.17.4
sannr *adj.* true I.2.3, I.24.1
sárr *adj.* sore I.16.4
sauðr *m.* sheep I.8.4
seggr *m.* (*poet.*) man II.18.1, III.17.3
segja *v.* to say I.1.3, I.4.1, I.15.3, I.23.1, II.22.1, III.17.3
seigr *adj.* tough, difficult II.2.3
sem *conj.* as I.9.1, I.18.3, II.9.1; as if I.11.4, III.4.2; who, which III.27.3
senda *v.* to send III.20.1

senn *adv.* all at once III.17.3

setja *v.* to place II.9.2, III.3.1, III.21.3, III.25.3

síðan *adv.* then II.3.3, III.3.1, III.24.3

síðr *adj.* long II.12.2

sigr *m.* victory I.12.2

sig *pron.* oneself III.10.3, III.15.3

sinn *pron.* his, hers, its III.18.1

sitja *v.* to sit III.8.2, III.15.2

sjálfr *adj.* self II.14.3, III.13.2

skaka *v.* to shake III.26.4

skálkr *m.* rogue III.26.2

skamm *f.* shame III.12.4

skegg *n.* beard III.22.4

skemmtan *f.* entertainment III.14.2

skíð *n.* long stave of wood II.12.1

skipa *v.* to arrange III.5.1

skorða *f.* support, prop II.3.1

skrúði *m.* raiment II.8.3

skulu *v.* shall, must I.17.4, I.18.3, II.4.1, II.8.2, II.8.3, II.13.2, II.20.2, III.1.1, III.20.2, III.27.4

slá *v.* to strike II.23.2

sléttr *adj.* smooth, flat I.22.2

slíkr *adj.* suchlike II.17.3, III.12.4

slyngr *adj.* clever III.1.4

slægð *f.* slyness, trickery I.4.2

slægr *adj.* sly III.2.2

smíða *v.* to smith, make through craft I.6.2

snekkja *f.* a type of ship II.1.1

sofa *v.* to sleep III.2.1, III.4.1

sorg *f.* sorrow I.15.3

sóti *m.* giant (*should perhaps be read as a proper noun* **Sóti**) II.21.2

spenna *v.* to span, gird I.9.3; to clasp II.6.1

spil *n.* game, play III.27.1

spjalla *v.* to speak, to chat II.23.1

spretta *v.* to spring up I.8.4

sprund *n.* (*poet.*) woman II.3.3

staðr *m.* place II.12.3

stærð *f.* size III.3.3

stál *n.* steel I.10.4

standa *v.* to stand I.21.3, II.16.2

steinn *m.* stone I.11.3, II.9.2

stórr *adj.* great, big I.3.2, I.4.4, I.12.1, I.13.1, III.8.1, III.22.1, III.25.2

strangr *adj.* painful, sore I.15.4

stundum *adv.* sometimes III.9.4

sundr *adv.* apart III.23.1, III.24.1

svá *adv.* thus, so I.25.4, III.2.3, III.9.1

svanr *m.* swan I.18.3

svara *v.* to reply III.12.2

svefn *m.* sleep I.13.2, II.5.3

sveipr *m.* (*here*) tumult III.7.4

sveit *f.* troop I.12.2, II.15.3, II.16.2, II.23.1, III.1.2, III.11.1

sækja *v.* to seek out, fetch III.20.2

sæmdargjarn *adj.* eager for honour II.18.1

sökkva *v.* to sink III.25.4

taka *v.* to take I.17.1, III.4.3, III.16.2, III.26.3; **taka** + *infinitive* to begin to do something I.13.1, I.16.4, I.23.2, II.7.3, III.11.1, III.17.3

tala *v.* to speak I.17.2, I.22.1, I.24.2, II.18.1, III.2.2, III.4.4, III.11.4, III.12.4, III.14.3

tár *n.* tear; **Gefnar tár** Gefn's tear > gold III.18.4

teitr *adj.* cheerful I.17.2, II.16.3

telja *v.* to count II.14.2
til *prep.* towards I.2.3, I.24.1, III.17.1
tími *m.* time, moment I.29.2
tjá *v.* to express, show I.27.1
tjalda *v.* to drape with cloth III.2.4
tólf *num.* twelve I.5.3, III.5.1, III.10.3, III.24.3
trúa *v.* to believe II.5.2, II.18.3
tröll *n.* troll I.7.3, II.14.2, III.4.3, III.24.3
töframaðr *m.* magician, male worker of magic II.14.13
tönn *f.* tooth III.24.4

úlfr *m.* wolf I.2.1, II.15.3
um *prep.* around, about III.9.2, III.12.4, III.27.3
undirheimr *m.* underworld I.18.4
undra *v.* to wonder at II.23.1, III.11.1
undra-digr *adj.* marvellously stout I.10.1
upp *prep.* upwards I.5.4, I.15.1, I.29.3, III.5.3, III.8.2, III.21.3, III.25.2
úr *prep.* out of II.6.2
út *adv.* outwards I.20.1, II.4.1
úti *adv.* outside I.21.3, II.16.2
uxi *m.* ox III.10.1

vagn *m.* wagon II.20.1
valda *v.* to be the cause of II.18.2
vanr *adj.* accustomed I.18.1
vargr *m.* wolf, *also used of criminals and outlaws* II.15.3
várr *pron.* ours III.18.3
vegr *m.* way I.20.2, I.29.4, II.11.2, II.13.2
veig *f.* strong drink II.2.1
veill *adj.* diseased, wretched I.22.1
veita *v.* to offer I.12.1, II.8.3, III.8.3

50 Þrymlur: The Bearded Bride

veizla *f.* feast II.17.1, III.3.2

vel *adv.* well I.3.1

vera *v.* to be; **væri** subjunctive form I.11.4

verða *v.* to become I.20.3, II.23.3, III.11.3, III.13.4, III.20.4; to be I.15.3, II.17.2, III.12.3

verr *adv.* worse III.5.4

versna *v.* to worsen III.23.3

vetr *m.* winter III.19.3

við, viðr *prep.* at II.6.3; with III.8.4; **viðr** *is an alternative form used in* III.22.3 *to rhyme with* niðr

víða *adv.* widely I.6.4

víf *n.* (*poet.*) woman I.25.2, II.19.3

vilja *v.* to want I.16.2, II.2.2, II.18.3, II.21.1, III.20.1; *auxiliary verb expressing futurity* II.9.1

villidýr *n.* wild animal II.15.2

vín *n.* wine III.23.2

vinna *v.* to perform, do I.11.1

vinr *m.* friend II.20.1

völlr *m.* field, plain II.7.1

völva *f.* fortune-teller, female worker of magic II.14.3

yfir *prep.* over I.20.1

ylgjast *v.* to frown II.6.3, II.20.2

ýtar *m.pl.* (*poet.*) men I.13.2, II.2.3, II.9.1, II.12.1

þá *conj.* then I.9.4, I.25.3

þangað *adv.* thither, to that place I.12.3

þannin *adv.* (*see also* **þannveg**) thus, so III.11.4

þannveg *adv.* (*see also* **þannin**) thus, so III.27.2

þar *adv.* there I.25.1, II.23.3, III.1.1, III.6.1, III.24.2

þegar *adv.* when, immediately I.7.1, I.9.3, II.19.3, III.15.2, III.17.1, III.25.4

þegn *m.* (*poet.*) man II.16.1, II.19.1, II.23.1, III.1.2

Glossary and Index of Names

þella *f.* a type of tree (pine?), *used in kenning for woman* II.2.1

þerna *f.* maidservant III.4.2

þiggja *v.* to receive II.3.2

þjónn *m.* servant I.21.1

þó *conj.* yet, nonetheless III.10.4, III.19.4, III.21.2, III.21.4

þorn *m.* brooch II.5.1

þrár *adj.* stubborn; **þrátt** frequently I.18.2

þrennr *num.* three, triple, threefold III.19.3

þriði *num.* third III.1.1

þrífa *v.* to catch hold of III.22.3

þrír *num.* three III.15.3

þrotinn *adj.* exhausted I.14.4

þrútinn *adj.* swollen II.5.1

þræll *m.* slave I.21.3, III.2.2

þungr *adj.* heavy I.7.4

þurs *m.* giant I.12.4, II.8.2, II.13.2, II.16.1, II.19.1, II.23.2

því *adv.* why II.17.1, II.22.2

þykkja *v. with dative subject* to seem I.19.1, II.6.2, II.10.3, II.19.2, III.1.4

þögn *f.* silence II.23.2

æða *v.* to rush furiously I.27.1

æsiligr *adj.* furious, violent III.25.1

öngvan *pron.* (*see also* **engi**) no one II.4.3

ör *f.* arrow I.10.1

INDEX OF NAMES

All proper nouns which appear in the text are given here in normalised form.

Ámr *m.* A giant. III.6.4.

Ása-Þórr *m.* A name for Þórr. I.4.3, II.8.1, II.12.1, II.17.1, III.25.3. See also: **Atli**, **Rymr**, **Þórr**.

Atli *m.* Þórr. I.6.1, II.5.2. See also: **Ása-Þórr**, **Rymr**, **Þórr**.

Baugi *m.* A name for Þrymr. III.3.2, III.16.3.

Besla *f.* A giantess. III.24.1.

Bil *f.* A goddess. III.17.2; **menja Bil** = woman.

Brúsi *m.* A name for Þrymr. II.22.1, III.14.3.

Brúsi *m.* As Þrymr is named elsewhere in this stanza, this presumably refers to a different giant. III.6.4.

Dofri *m.* A name for Þrymr. I.24.2.

Dofri *m.* As Þrymr is named elsewhere in this stanza, this presumably refers to a different giant. III.6.4.

Eitri *m.* A dwarf. I.6.1.

Fala *f.* A giantess. III.7.2.

Fenrisúlfr *m.* One of Loki's monstrous offspring. I.2.1.

Freyja *f.* One of the Ásynjur. I.15.1, I.16.1, I.25.1, I.28.3, I.29.3, II.1.3, II.22.2, III.2.3, III.13.2.

Fríðr *f.* A woman's name. II.12.3. **Fríðr hringa** = woman.

Fjölnir *m.* A name for Óðinn. I.21.1, II.1.4. **Fjölnis þjónn** = Loki. **Fjölnis burr** = Þórr.

Gefn *f.* A woman's name. II.5.1, III.18.4; **þorna Gefn** = woman. **Gefnar tár** = gold.

Geitir *m.* A giant. III.6.3.

Gjálp *f.* A giantess. III.7.3.

Glámr *m.* A giant. III.6.3.

Gleipnir *m.* The dwarf-made girdle used to bind Fenrisúlfr until Ragnarök. I.2.2.

Glossary and Index of Names

Greip *f.* A giantess. III.7.3.

Gríðr *f.* A giantess. III.7.2.

Grímnir *m.* A name for Óðinn. I.10.3. **Grímnis kundr** = Þórr.

Grímnir *m.* A name for Þrymr. II.19.2.

Grímnir *m.* This occurs in a list of giant names; as Þrymr is named elsewhere in the stanza, it presumably refers to a different giant. III.6.4.

Hafli *m.* A giant, possibly Þrymr's cook. III.16.2.

Haki *m.* A giant. III.6.1.

Heimdæll *m.* One of the Æsir. I.8.1, II.10.1.

Hel *f.* One of Loki's monstrous offspring; she rules a realm of the dead. I.3.3.

Herjann *m.* A name for Óðinn. I.5.2, II.1.1. **Herjans burr** = Þórr.

Hlökk *f.* A giantess. III.7.3.

Hrymr *m.* A giant. III.6.1

Hænir *m.* One of the Æsir. II.10.1.

Keila *f.* A giantess. III.21.3.

Lóður *m.* A name for Loki. I.22.3.

Loki *m.* One of the Æsir. I.1.2, I.3.3, I.4.1, I.18.1, I.19.4, I.23.2, II.10.2. See also: **Lóður**, **Loftr**.

Loftr *m.* A name for Loki. I.1.4, I.19.3, III.1.3, III.4.1, III.12.1.

Mjöllnir *m.* Þórr's dwarf-made hammer. I.6.3, I.7.4, I.13.3, I.23.3, I.27.4, II.6.1, III.22.3.

Móði *m.* A giant. III.6.3.

Óðinn *m.* One of the Æsir. I.3.1, I.4.3, II.7.1, II.11.1, III.2.2. **Óðins son** = Þórr. **Óðins þræll** = Loki. See also: **Fjölnir**, **Grímnir**, **Herjann**, **Rögnir**.

Ofnir *m.* A serpent. II.12.1. **Ofnis skíð** = gold.

Rymr *m.* A name for Þórr. II.6.3, III.26.2.

Rögnir *m.* A name for Óðinn. I.26.2, I.29.1, II.7.2. **Rögnis kundr** = Þórr.

Sauðungr *m.* A name for Þrymr. III.25.3.

Sleipnir *m.* Óðinn's eight-legged horse, which Loki gave birth to while in the form of a mare. I.2.4.

Surtr *m.* A giant. III.6.1.

Syrpa *f.* A giantess. III.7.3, III.20.1.

Sörkvir *m.* A giant. III.6.3.

Ullr *m.* One of the Æsir. I.1.1.

Þórr *m.* One of the Æsir. I.13.3, I.15.2, I.23.3, II.5.1, III.8.2, III.22.2.

Þrymr *m.* A giant. I.12.3, I.21.4, II.19.1, II.23.1, III.6.2, III.18.1, III.26.2. See also: **Dofri**, **Grímnir**, **Brúsi**, **Baugi**, **Suðungr**.

Þundar *m.pl.* Apparently the name of Þrymr's estate. II.16.1.

Þundr *m.* A name for Óðinn, here used in a kenning for Þórr. I.10.1.

örva-Þundr = Þórr.

MANUSCRIPTS

This list includes all manuscripts referred to in the Introduction and Notes.

AM 604 g 4to

AM 721 4to

AM 972 a 4to

GKS 1005 fol.

GKS 2397 4to

KB Vs 20

Kollsbók = Codex Guelferbytanus 42. 7. Augusteus quarto. Facsimile edition in Ólafur Halldórsson (1968). Íslenzk handrit, series in quarto V. Handritastofnun Íslands, Reykjavík.

NKS 815 b 4to

NKS 1568 4to

Bibliography

Aðalsteinn Hákonarson 2016. 'Aldur tvíhljóðunar í forníslensku'. *Íslenskt mál* 38, 83–123.
Ármann Jakobsson 2014. 'The Homer Of The North or: who was Sigurður the Blind?' *European Journal of Scandinavian Studies* 44:1, 4–19.
Björn K. Þórólfsson 1934. *Rímur fyrir 1600*. Copenhagen: Hið íslenska fræðafjelag.
Björn K. Þórólfsson 1950. 'Dróttkvæði og rímur. Að stofni til erindi flutt í Vísindafélagi Íslendinga, 21. janúar 1947'. *Skírnir* 124, 175–209.
Boberg, Inger Margrethe 1966. *Motif-Index of Early Icelandic Literature*. Bibliotheca Arnamagnæana XXVII. Copenhagen: Munksgaard.
Bugge, Sophus and Moltke Moe, eds, 1897. *Torsvisen i sin norske form*. Christiana: Centraltrykkeriet.
Clunies Ross, Margaret 2001. 'Reading *Þrymskviða*'. In *The Poetic Edda: Essays on Old Norse Mythology*,. Ed. Paul Acker and Carolyne Larrington. London, New York: Routledge, 177–94.
DgF = Svend Grundtvig, ed., 1966. *Danmarks Gamle Folkeviser*. Vols. 1 and 4. 2nd edition. Copenhagen: Universitets-Jubilæets Danske Samfund.

Eddukvæði = Jónas Kristjánsson and Vésteinn Ólason, eds, 2014. *Eddukvæði* I. *Goðakvæði*. Íslenzk fornrit. Reykjavik: Hið íslenzka fornritafélag.

Eggert Ólafsson and Bjarni Pálsson 1772. *Vice-Lavmand Eggert Olassens og Land-Physici Biarne Povelsens Reise igiennem Island* I. Copenhagen: Videnskabernes Selskæb.

Faulkes, Anthony, ed., 2005. *Snorri Sturluson. Edda. Prologue and Gylfaginning.* London: Viking Society for Northern Research.

Faulkes, Anthony, ed., 2007. *Snorri Sturluson. Edda. Skáldskaparmál* 1. London: Viking Society for Northern Research.

Finnur Jónsson 1896. *Fernir fornislenzkir rímnaflokkar.* Copenhagen: S. L. Møller.

Finnur Jónsson 1920. *Den oldnorske og oldislandske litteraturs historie* 3. Copenhagen: G. E. C. Gads Forlag.

Finnur Jónsson 1926–28. *Ordbog til de af Samfund til udg. af gml. nord. litteratur udgivne rímur samt til de af dr. O. Jiriczek udgivne Bósarimur.* Copenhagen: J. Jørgensen and Co. (Ivar Jantzen).

Finnur Sigmundsson 1966. *Rímnatal.* Reykjavik: Rímnafélagið.

Flateyjarbók I 1944. Akranes: Flateyjarútgáfan.

Frog 2011. 'Circum-Baltic Mythology? The Strange Case of the Theft of the Thunder-Instrument (ATU 1148b)'. *Archaeologia Baltica* 15, 78–98.

Gras, E. J. 1931. *De noordse Loki-mythen in hun onderling verband.* Haarlem: D. Tjeenk Willink and Zoon.

Grüner Nielsen, Hakon 1911. 'Torsvisen på Færøerne'. *Maal og Minne*, 72–76.

Gunnell, Terry 1995. *The Origins of Drama in Scandinavia.* Cambridge: D. S. Brewer.

Gurevich, Elena, ed., 2017a. *Anonymous Þulur: Dverga heiti.* In *Poetry from Treatises on Poetics. Skaldic Poetry of the Scandinavian Middle Ages* 3. Ed. Kari Ellen Gade and Edith Marold. Turnhout: Brepols, 692–706.

Gurevich, Elena, ed., 2017b. *Anonymous Þulur: Óðins nǫfn.* In *Poetry from Treatises on Poetics. Skaldic Poetry of the Scandinavian Middle Ages* 3. Ed. Kari Ellen Gade and Edith Marold. Turnhout: Brepols, 731–53.

Gurevich, Elena, ed., 2017c. *Anonymous Þulur: Þórs heiti.* In *Poetry from Treatises on Poetics. Skaldic Poetry of the Scandinavian Middle Ages* 3. Ed. Kari Ellen Gade and Edith Marold. Turnhout: Brepols, 758–60.

Hallfreður Örn Eiríksson 1975. 'On Icelandic Rímur: An Orientation'. *Arv* 31, 139–50.

Harris, Joseph 2012. 'Eddic Poetry and the Ballad Voice'. In *Child's Children. Ballad Study and its Legacies.* Ed. Joseph Harris and Barbara Hillers. Trier: Wissenschaftlicher Verlag Trier, 155–70.

Haukur Þorgeirsson 2013. *Hljóðkerfi og bragkerfi. Stoðhljóð, tónkvæði og önnur úrlausnarefni í íslenskri bragsögu ásamt útgáfu á Rímum af Ormari Fraðmarssyni.* Ph. D. thesis, University of Iceland.

Heide, Eldar 2011. 'Loki, the Vätte, and the Ash Lad: A Study Combining Old Scandinavian and Late Material'. *Viking and Medieval Scandinavia* 7, 63–106.

Hughes, Shaun 1978. '"Völsunga rímur" and "Sjúrðar kvæði": Romance and Ballad, Ballad and Dance'. In *Ballads and Ballad Research: Selected Papers of the International Conference on Nordic and Anglo-American Ballad Research:*

University of Washington, Seattle, May 2–6, 1977. Ed. Patricia Conroy. Seattle: University of Washington Press, 37–45.
Hughes, Shaun 2005. 'Late Secular Poetry'. In *A Companion to Old Norse-Icelandic Literature and Culture*. Ed. Rory McTurk. Oxford: Blackwell, 205–22.
ÍM = Jón Helgason, ed., 1936–38. *Íslenzk miðaldakvæði* I–II. Copenhagen: Kommissionen for det Arnamagnæanske legat.
Jiriczek, Otto Luitpold, ed., 1893. *Die Bósa-saga in zwei Fassungen nebst Proben aus den Bósa-rímur*. Strassburg: Verlag von Karl J. Trübner.
Jón Helgason 1975. 'Noter til Þrymlur'. *Opuscula* 5, 241–49.
Jonsson, Bengt R. 1991. 'Oral Literature, Written Literature: The Ballad and Old Norse Genres'. In *The Ballad and Oral Literature*. Ed. Joseph Harris. Cambridge, MA: Harvard University Press, 139–70.
Jonsson, Bengt R., Margareta Jersild and Sven-Bertil Jansson, eds, 2001. *Sveriges Medeltida Ballader* 5:1. Stockholm: Almqvist and Wiksell International.
Jorgensen, Peter 1993. 'Rímur'. In *Medieval Scandinavia: An Encyclopedia*. Ed. Phillip Pulsiano and Kirsten Wolf. New York and London: Garland, 536–37.
Karl Óskar Ólafsson 2006. *'Þrír feðgar hafa skrifað bók þessa—'. Um þrjár rithendur í AM 510 4to og fleiri handritum*. M. A. thesis, University of Iceland.
Kuhn, Hans 1990–93. 'The *rímur*-poet and his audience'. *Saga-Book* XXIII, 454–68.
Kölbing, Eugen 1884. *Amis and Amiloun zugleich mit der altfranzösischen Quelle*. Heilbronn: Verlag von Gebr. Henninger.
Lassen, Annette 2003. *Øjet og blindheden i norrøn litteratur og mythologi*. Copenhagen: Museum Tusculanums Forlag.
de Leeuw van Weenen, Andrea 2000. *A Grammar of Möðruvallabók*. Leiden: Research School CNWS, Universiteit Leiden.
Louis-Jensen, Jonna 1992. 'Om Ólíf og Landrés, vers og prosa samt kvinder og poeter'. In *Eyvindarbók: Festskrift til Eyvind Fjeld Halvorsen*. Ed. Finn Hødnebø et al. Oslo: Institutt for nordistikk og litteraturvitenskap, 217–30.
McKinnell, John 2014. 'Myth as Therapy: The Usefulness of *Þrymskviða*'. In *Essays on Eddic Poetry*. Ed. Donata Kick and John D. Shafer. Toronto: University of Toronto Press, 200–20.
Meulengract Sorensen, Preben 1983. *The Unmanly Man: Concepts of Sexual Defamation in Early Northern Society*. Odense: Odense University Press.
Möbius, Theodor 1860. *Edda Sæmundar hins fróða mit einem Anhang zum Theil bisher ungedruckter Gedichte*. Leipzig: J. C. Hinrichs'sche Buchhandlung.
Niles, John D. 1999. *Homo Narrans. The Poetics and Anthropology of Oral Literature*. Philadelphia: University of Pennsylvania Press.
Oddur Einarsson 1928. *Qualiscunque Descriptio Islandiae*. Ed. Fritz Burg. Hamburg: Selbstverlag der Staats- und Universitäts-Bibliothek.
Ólafur Halldórsson, ed., 1973. *Haralds rímur Hringsbana*. Reykjavik: Stofnun Árna Magnússonar á Íslandi.
Ólafur Halldórsson, ed., 1974. *Bósa rímur*. Reykjavik: Stofnun Árna Magnússonar á Íslandi.

Ólafur Halldórsson, ed., 1975. *Vilmundar rímur viðutan*. Reykjavik: Stofnun Árna Magnússonar á Íslandi.
Paret, Rudi 1930. *Die legendäre Maghazi-literatur*. Tübingen: J. C. B. Mohr.
Ragnar Ingi Aðalsteinsson 2014. *Traditions and Continuities. Alliteration in Old and Modern Icelandic Verse*. Reykjavik: University of Iceland Press.
RR = Theodor Wisén, ed., 1881. *Riddara-rímur*. Copenhagen: F. Berling.
Rs = Finnur Jónsson, ed., 1905–22. *Rímnasafn. Samling af de ældste islandske rimer* I–II. Copenhagen: S. L. Møller.
Sanders, Christopher, ed., 2000. *Tales of Knights: Perg. fol. nr 7 in The Royal Library, Stockholm (AM 567 VI β 4to, NKS 1265 IIc fol.)*. Manuscripta Nordica 1. Copenhagen: C. A. Reitzel.
Schott, Christine M. 2010. *Footnotes on Life. Marginalia in Three Medieval Icelandic Manuscripts*. M. A. thesis, University of Iceland.
Singer, Samuel 1932. 'Die Grundlagen der *Thrymskvidha*'. *Neophilologus* 17, 47–48.
Stefán Karlsson 1970. 'Um Vatnshyrnu'. *Opuscula* IV, 279–303.
Sverrir Tómasson 2000. '"Strákligr líz mér Skíði." *Skíðaríma* – Íslenskur föstuleikur?' *Skírnir* 174, 305–20.
Sverrir Tómasson 2012. 'The Function of Rímur in Iceland during the Late Middle Ages'. In *Balladen-Stimmen. Vokalität als theoretisches und historisches Phänomen*, 59–74. Ed. Jürg Glauser. Tübingen: Francke.
University of Copenhagen. 'The ballad books'. Danish Under Digital Study. Accessed 19th July 2017. http://duds.nordisk.ku.dk/english/digital-text-archives/oldest_danish_ballad-tradition/viseboegerne/
University of Oslo. 'Torekall vinn att hamaren sin'. Dokumentationsprojekt. Accessed 11th July 2017. http://www.dokpro.uio.no/ballader/tekster_html/e/e126_001.html
Uther, Hans-Jörg 2004. *The Types of International Folktales. A Classification and Bibliography. Part I*. Helsinki: Academia Scientiarum Fennica.
Vésteinn Ólason 1982. *The Traditional Ballads of Iceland: Historical Studies*. Reykjavik: Stofnun Árna Magnússonar á Íslandi.
Vijūnas, Aurelijus 2019. 'Problems in Mythological Reconstruction: Thor, Thrym, and the Story of the Hammer over the Course of Time'. Forthcoming.
Wilson, John, ed., 1953. *Samsons saga fagra*. Samfund til udgivelse af gammal nordisk literatur. Copenhagen: SUGNL.
Þorvaldur Sigurðsson 1986. *Sigurðar rímur þögla*. M. A. thesis, University of Iceland.